The true significance of man as a picture-maker must rest within the pictures that he chooses to make, and not by any verbal construct we may impose upon them. For many picture-makers, preconceptions about the photographic medium seem less significant at this time than they have in the past. These changes in visual attitudes do not necessarily suggest a greater degree of significance, but rather a shifting of the terms needed to explore those enigmatic problems of assimilating the experience of an individual or a culture.

VISION AND EXPRESSION continues a series of visual books intended to survey the work of a younger generation of photographers. The designation "younger" does not refer to chronological age, but to attitude. It may also be evident that the suggestion "younger" does not imply difference as it relates to stylistic or thematic position, but intensity and concern. An objective evaluation of the work might declare the terms by which we may effectively begin to understand the meaning of the limitations, as well as the possible extensions, of photography as it relates to human expression. On one level the photographs in this present book are intentionally ordered to provide a range of comparatives to discuss the many aspects of the photographers' visual vocabulary.

The method of selection bears mentioning. The 154 plates were chosen from over 6000 photographs. Over 1200 photographers submitted five to ten photographs each of recent work. The only stipulation was that no photographer who had been included in our previous survey, PHOTOGRAPHY 63, could submit work to this current exhibition, thus achieving one aspect of the program—a continuing directory of contemporary photographers. A preliminary sorting was achieved by members of the Staff of the George Eastman House. This first stage functioned as a control on my own reactions by minimizing the possibility of set responses on my part. With the aid of one staff member, all groups were reviewed again and again for a period of one week before any work was rejected. The primary reference was each photograph in relation to photographs within the group the photographer submitted, and then its relationship as a group to the work of other photographers being considered. If, at any point, I hesitated in making a decision, the work was set aside and reviewed again on the following day or, as in many cases, days. The procedure took almost three months and, quite often, to the dismay of my colleagues, the preliminary groupings were altered radically. While the process was essentially non-verbal, the questioning became intense. Have I understood the photographer's concern? Is it articulate? On what terms? Is his work consistent, inconsistent, vague, or generative? How does it compare . . .?

If then this book were to be representative of picture-making concerns, the condition of selection had to be based upon my awareness of intent, determined by the conditions of the photographer's work and not by any external preconceptions.

The attempt should only be considered preliminary, but the intention should begin to raise a number of questions regarding the procedural position of an institution in relation to its medium's practitioners. The active product of the picture-maker must not be inhibited by meaningless ritual, but should be approached through self-clarification.

Institutional activity should exist in support of the photographer's direct commitment, not as sanctioner, but to extend the dialogue of his work to others. Utopian as the position may seem, it can afford a range of rather interesting options in clarifying the possibilities of vision and expression through photography.

Index

Elly Gordon 128
Untitled, 1968.
[Kodalith print] 3¾ x 5½"

Emmett Gowin II 49
Edith with Sister, Danville, Virginia, 1966.
5 x 6¼"

Betty Hahn 71
Girl with 4 Roads, 1968. [Color, gum bichromate print] 14½ x 21½"

Robert F. Haiko 15
Kemp's Television, 1967. 4¾ x 7¼"

Zdeněk Halámek 132
Nostalgia, ca. 1967. 7 x 9¼"

Chauncey Hare 73
Home in a Basement, Berkeley, 1968.
8¾ x 12¼"

Pamela Harris-McLeod 19
Mountain Family,
Decoy, Kentucky, 1966. 9¾ x 6½"

Robert Häusser 31
From the series: "home slaughtering in the country," ca. 1967. 24 x 18½"

R. Eugene Hayes 50
Dark Bush, 1968. 7½ x 8¾"

Robert F. Heinecken 138
Four Costumes, 1968. [Color, photomontage with film overlay] 9½ x 15"

Reginald Heron 141
Rochester #2, 1967. 5¾ x 4¼"

Warren M. Hill 140
Compartmental Series, 1967. 9 x 18"

Bradley Hindson 90
Burlesque Lady With Monkey, 1967.
6¼ x 9½"

Walter Hirsch 39
London, 1968. 13½ x 9¼"

Hisae Imai 154
Open-Air Creatures, 1965. 10 x 9¾"

Brian M. Jacobs 136
Vivian, 1968. [Plexiglas construction]
14¼ x 12¼ x 4"

Håkan Johansson 41
Astronautenlook, 1967. 15¾ x 10½"

Harold H. Jones III 105
From the series: "untitled poems to the sky," 1968. [Applied color] 6 x 5¾"

Jo Diane Kasper 124
Self Portrait #2, 1967. 9¾ x 7"

Bruce Katsiff 133
Untitled, 1968. 30 x 24"

Kikuji Kawada 29
Wax Museum, New York, 1967.
7¼ x 11"

Dennis C. Kievets 142
Avatar I, 1966. 7½ x 9½"

Rosalind S. Kimball 55
Untitled, 1967. 9½ x 7½"

Irwin B. Klein 26
David in the Mansion El Rito,
New Mexico, 1967. 9 x 13½"

Jim Kraft 149
Honeys IV:2, 1968. [Transparency-overlay, with applied color] 8¾ x 6¾"

Arthur Kramer 72
Untitled, 1967. 3¼ x 4¾"

Leslie R. Krims 59
Untitled, 1967. [Kodalith print]
7¼ x 10½"

Paul Krot 103
1-4, 1968. 80 x 120"

Kunié 121
From the series: "CKO," 1967. [Color]
10¼ x 13¼"

Tatsuo Kurihara 150
A Collier in Snowstorm, 1968.
10¼ x 14¼"

William G. Larson 134
Grace and Arthur, 1968.
[Color] 2¼ x 18"

Nick Lawrence 47
Henry, Freddie, Gilbert, 1967. 10¾ x 15"

Robert Lebeck 14
Robert Kennedy Funeral, 1968.
15¾ x 23¼"

James Lemkin 92
Dansville Hotel, Dansville,
New York, 1968. 6 x 9"

Joanne Leonard 18
Untitled, 1967. 5¾" in diameter.

Jacquelin Livingston 102
Transposition #2, 1967. 7¼ x 6¾"

Rocco M. Lodise 69
Untitled, 1968. 9¾ x 7½"

Ronald L. MacNeil 61
Untitled, 1966. 9½ x 7½"

Alen MacWeeney 151
Tinkers: Child in a Caravan, 1966.
7¾ x 11½"

Jerald C. Maddox 65
Figure IV, 1968. 9½ x 7¾"

Mary Ellen Mark 27
Girl in Trabzon, Turkey, 1965. 13 x 8½"

Michael McLoughlin 91
Untitled, 1967. 5¼ x 8"

Larry McPherson 96
Side of House,
Rochester, 1966. 6¼ x 5"

Roger Mertin 115
From the series: "Plastic Love-Dream,"
1968. 4 x 7¼"

Ronald Mesaros 93
Vesta, 1966. 5½ x 8"

Gary Metz 112
From the portfolio: "Song of the Shirt,"
1967, in collaboration with John Moore.
[Color, photo-offset lithograph] 5 x 7½"

Joel Meyerowitz 43
Spain, 1967. 9 x 13¼"

Chester J. Michalik 24
Untitled, 1967. 6½ x 6½"

Duane Michals 53
Dead Man, 1967. 7¾ x 5¼"

John Mills 64
Venus #2, 1968. 9¾ x 7½"

Stephen Mindel 68
For Allen Ginsberg, 1968.
[Applied color] 10 x 8"

David S. Moy 77
Untitled, 1968. 4¾ x 7"

Rodney Mullen 74
MacElroy Street, Oakland,
California, 1968. 7¾ x 11¼"

Stephen S. Myers 58
Untitled, 1967.
[Kodalith print] 7¾ x 5¼"

Henry Wessel, Jr.

J. Douglas Stewart

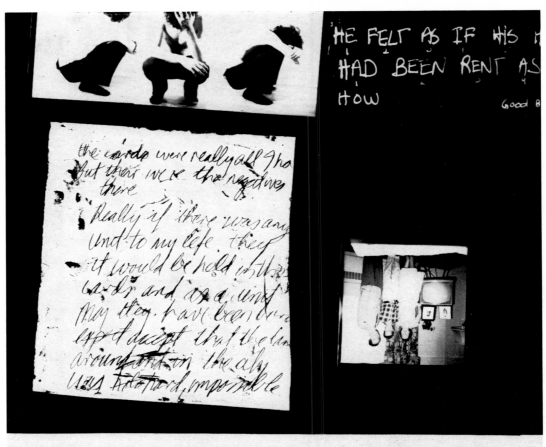

Teddy Newman

Burk Uzzle

Benedict J. Fernandez

Robert Lebeck

Robert F. Haiko

Linn Sage

Neil Beitzell

Joanne Leonard

Pamela Harris-McLeod

Robert D'Alessandro

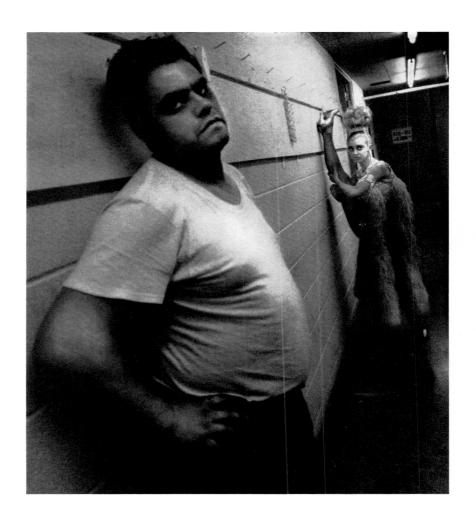

Michel Saint-Jean

Wolf von dem Bussche

Leif Skoogfors

Chester J. Michalik

Egons Spuris

Irwin B. Klein

Mary Ellen Mark

Arthur Tress

Kikuji Kawada

Tony Ray-Jones

Robert Häusser

EPC 235

Nina Raginsky

Jill Freedman

Pavel Vácha

Jiří Erml

Murray Riss

Judy Dater

Tod Papageorge

Walter Hirsch

Carl Fleischhauer

Håkan Johansson

Walter Rabetz

Joel Meyerowitz

Bart Parker

Richard Gates

Linda S. Connor

Nick Lawrence

Anders Petersen

Emmet Gowin II

R. Eugene Hayes

Paul J. Wigger

David Batchelder

Duane Michals

Eugene Edward Richards

Rosalind S. Kimball

Mark Cohen

Myron Wood

Stephen S. Myers

Leslie R. Krims

Antonio A. Fernandez

Ronald L. MacNeil

Maureen Bisilliat

Donald J. Erceg

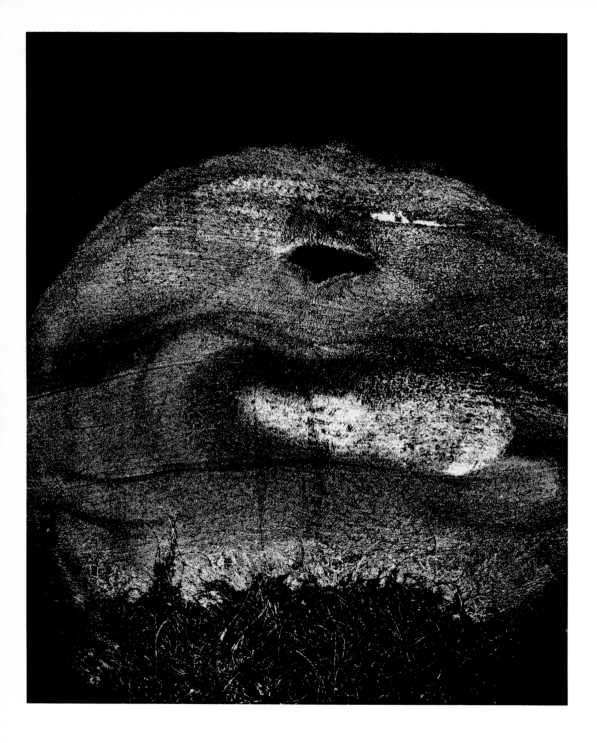

John Mills

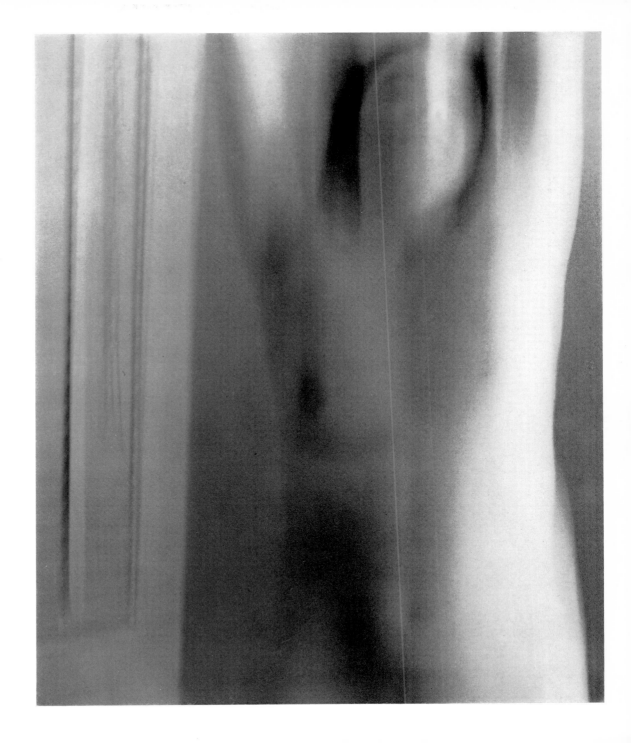

Jerald C. Maddox

Donald Blumberg

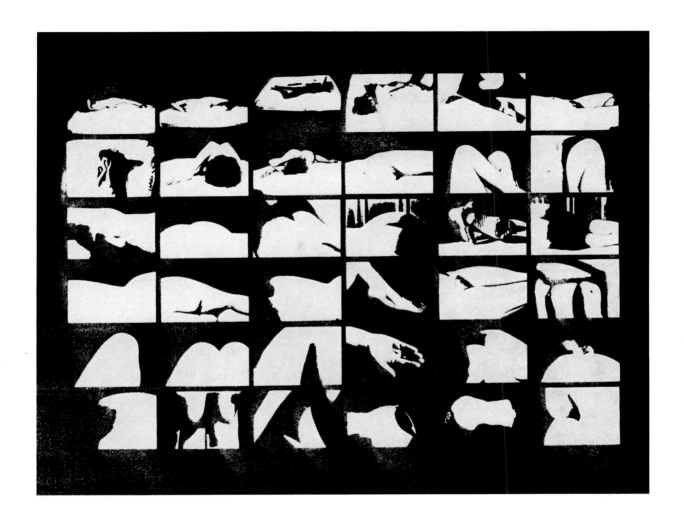

Pierre Cordier

Stephen Mindel

Rocco M. Lodise

Lawrence L. Simon

Betty Hahn

Arthur Kramer

Chauncey Hare

Rodney Mullen

Steven D. Foster

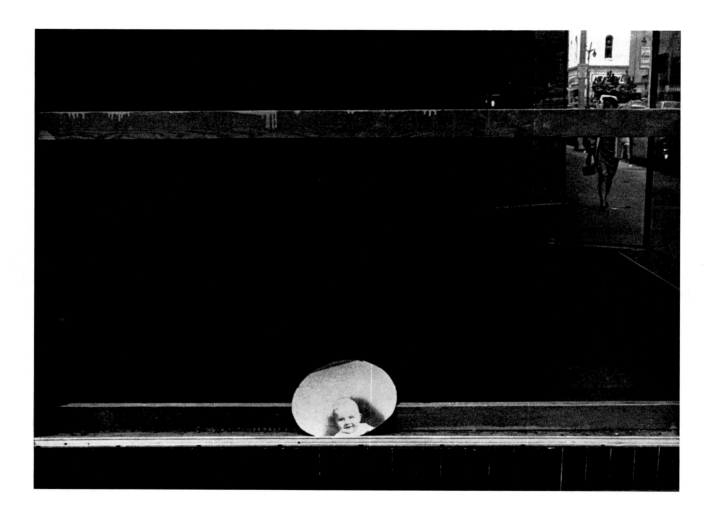

Gordon Bennett

David S. Moy

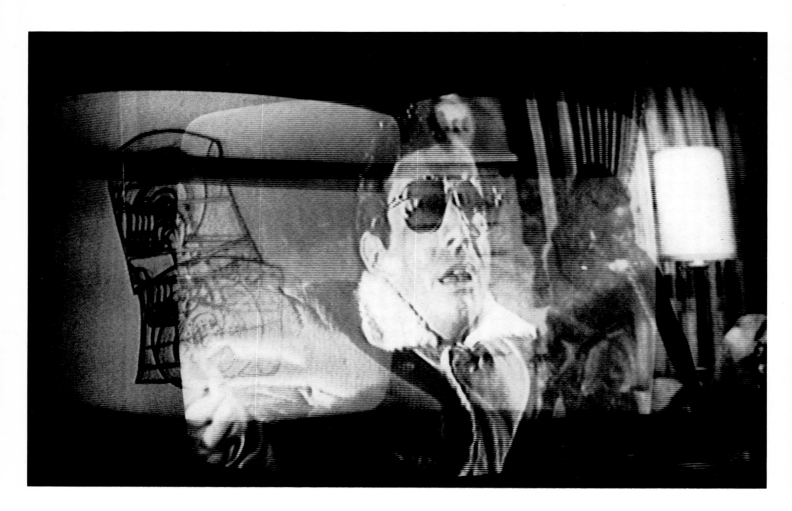

Thomas F. Barrow

David Vestal

Dean Brown

Waclaw Nowak

Gary Viskupic

Leland D. Rice

Fred Parker

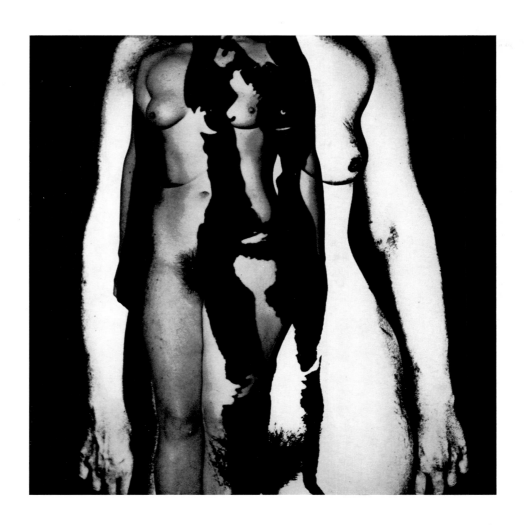

Jack F. Wilgus

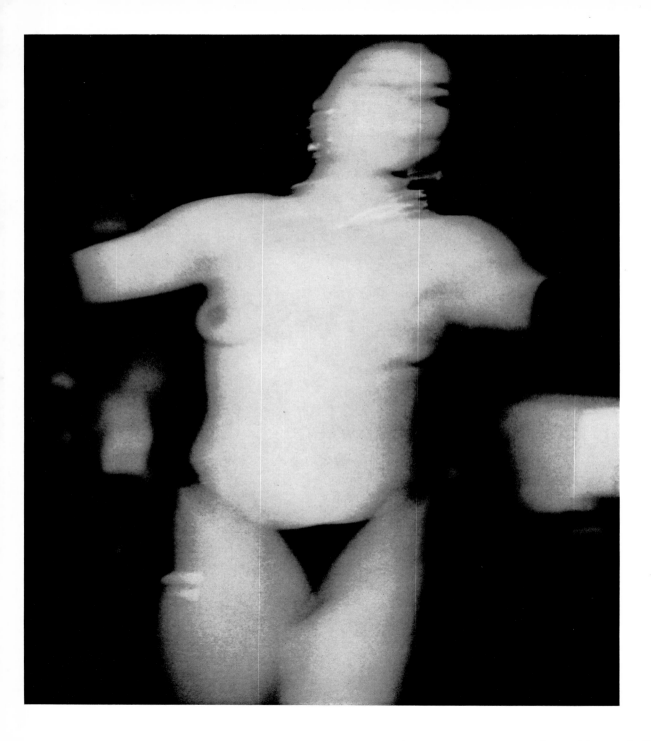

Ron Testa

William Gedney

Tom Zimmermann

Ellen Epstein

Bradley Hindson

Michael McLoughlin

James Lemkin

Ronald Mesaros

Donald Wright Patterson, Jr.

Thomas Porett

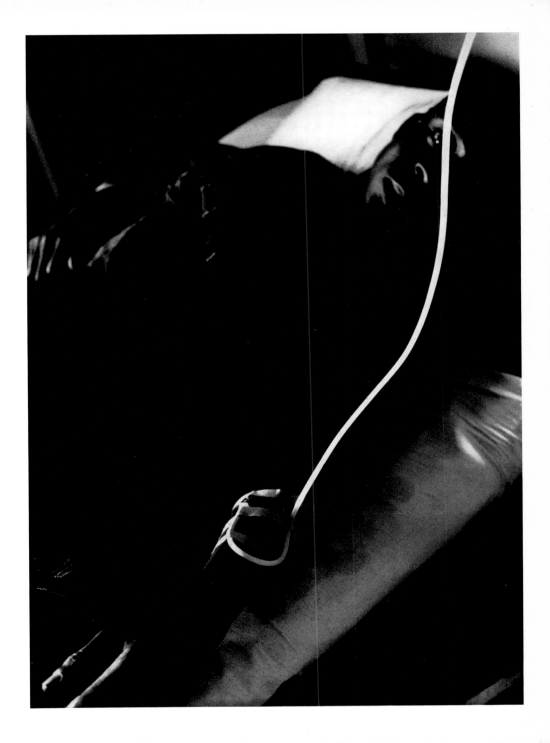

Michael Semak

Larry McPherson

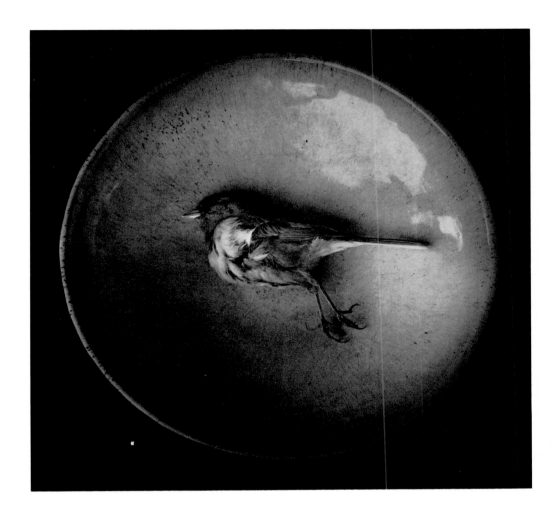

Phil Palmer

Kurt W. Erben

Michael Bishop

David Pilbrow

Thomas Cugini

Jacquelin Livingston

Paul Krot

Haruo Tomiyama

Harold H. Jones III

Geoffrey L. Winningham

James Newberry

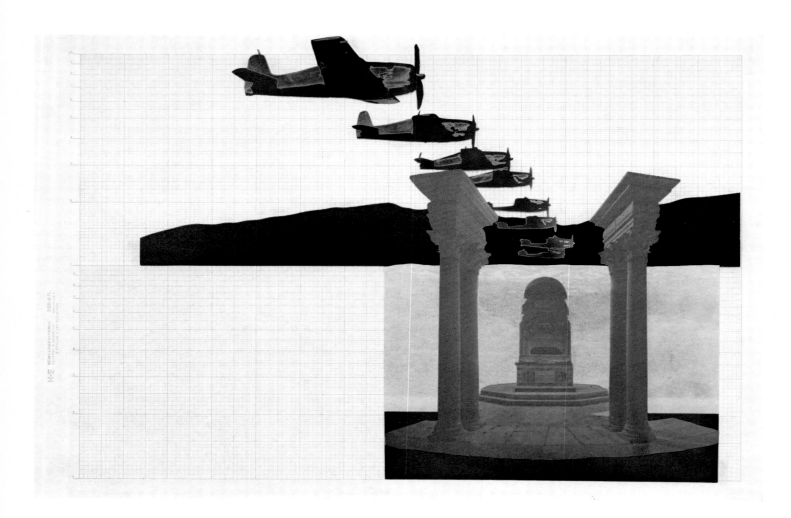

Carl Cheng

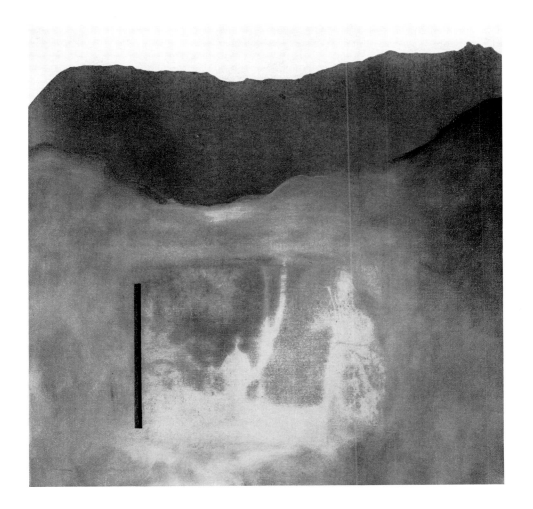

Donald Dickinson

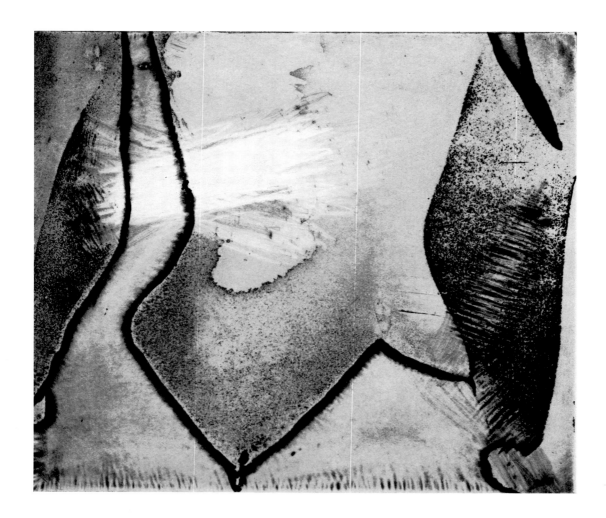

Alvin Rosenbaum

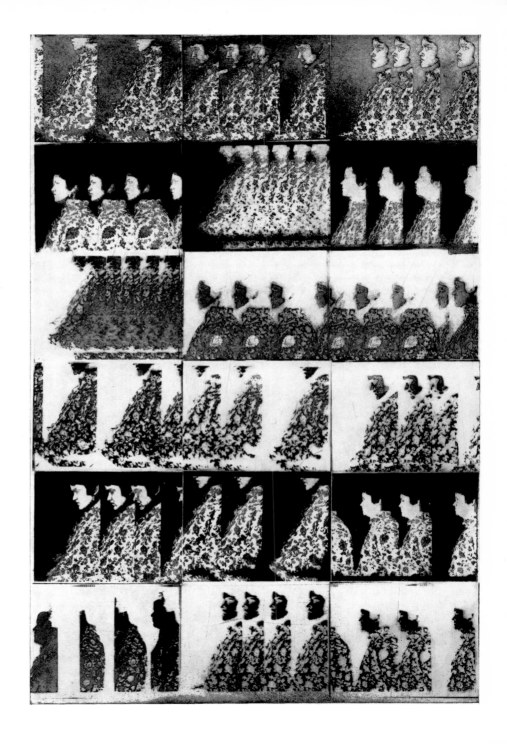

Keith A. Smith

Gary Metz

Charles Compère

Serge A. Scherbatskoy

Roger Mertin

Floris Michael Neusüss

Michael J. Teres

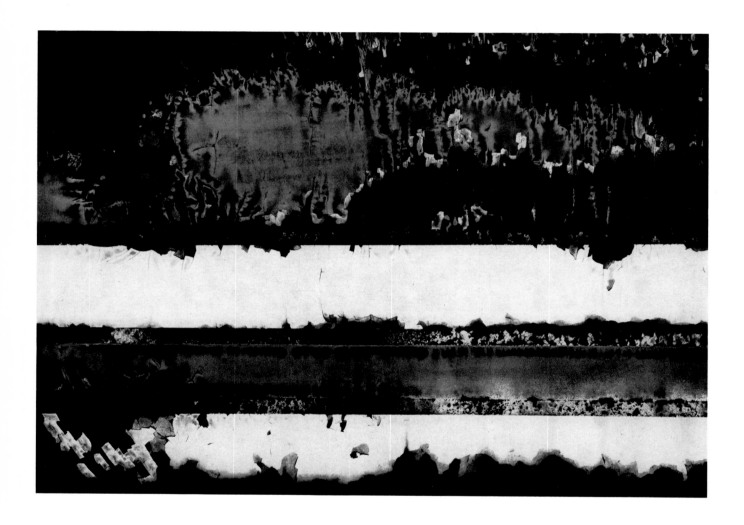

Michael Becotte

Philip L. Smith

Ann Warrington Wills

Kunié

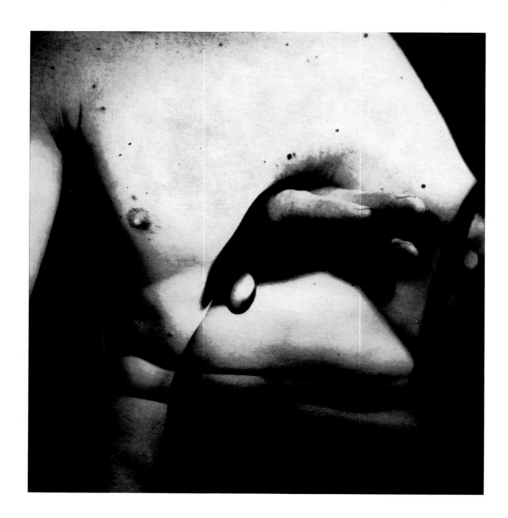

Robin Panda

Barry Burlison

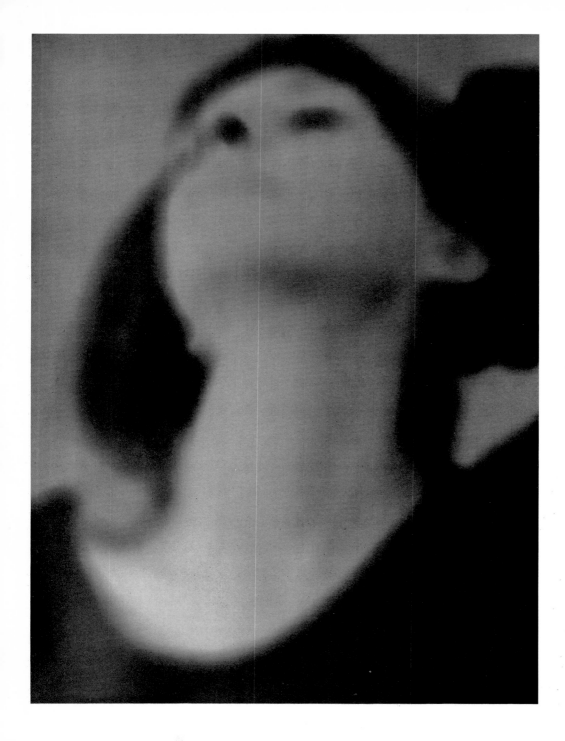

Jo Diane Kasper

John Spence Weir

David F. Banks

Jon Ellis Stevens

Elly Gordon

Robert Risager

Ladislaus Borodáč

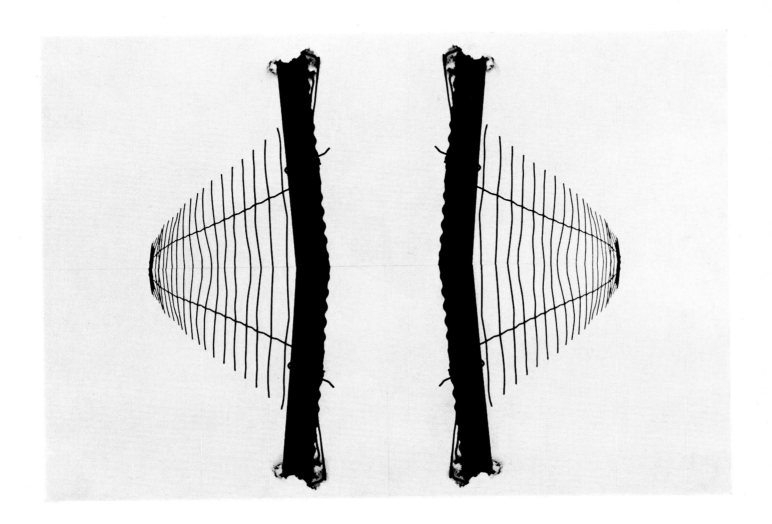

William A. Winans

Zdeněk Halámek

Bruce Katsiff

134

William G. Larson

Barbara Blondeau

Frank Salmo

Brian M. Jacobs

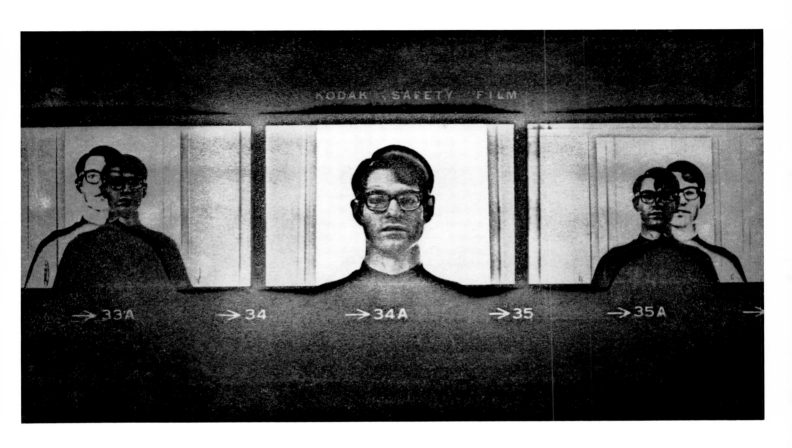

James Fallon

Robert F. Heinecken

Joyce Neimanas

Warren M. Hill

Reginald Heron

Dennis C. Kievets

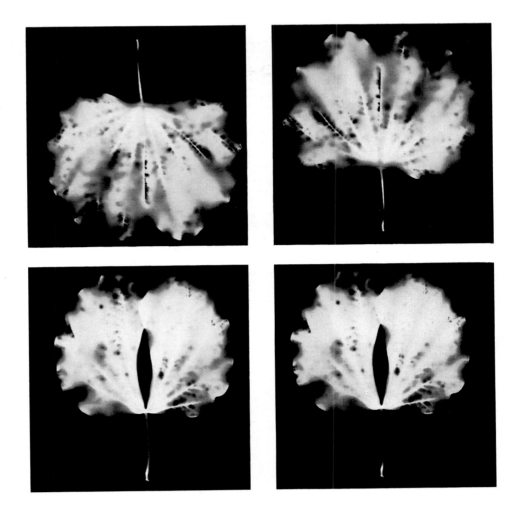

Chuck Fridenmaker

Oliver L. Gagliani

James Alinder

Robert E. Brown

Darryl J. Curran

Roslyn Banish

Stanley Blanchard

Jim Kraft

Tatsuo Kurihara

Alen MacWeeney

Clyde Dilley

Brian Pelletier

Hisae Imai

Larry Colwell

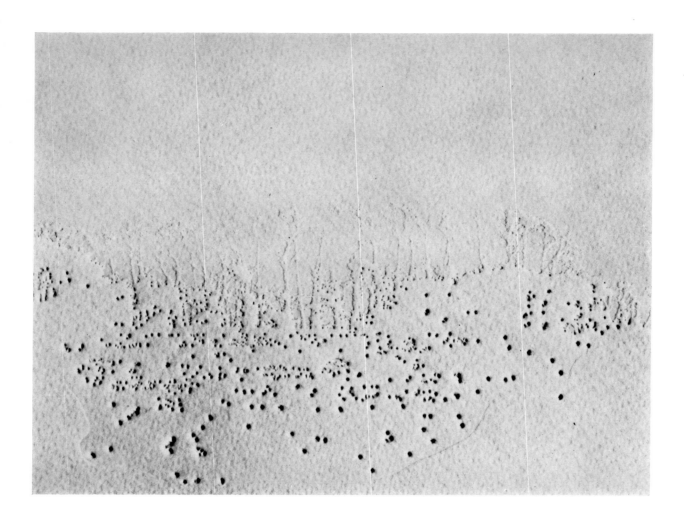

David Colley

David Ruether

Takayuki Ogawa

John Wood

James Alinder born Glendale, California, 1941. Received B.A. degree, Macalester College, 1962. Studied: University of Minnesota, 1962-64. Peace Corps volunteer to Somali Republic, East Africa, 1964-66. Received M.F.A. degree, University of New Mexico, Albuquerque, 1968. Photographs published: *Photography Annual,* 1968, 1969; *Aperture,* 14:1 (1968); *A History of East and Central Africa* (Longman & Green, 1968); *Horn of Africa: The Somali Republic* (in press); *Woman,* 1969. One-man exhibitions: University of Maine, Orono, 1968; "Somali Photographs," University of Nebraska at Omaha, 1969. Two-man exhibition: Quivera Gallery, Corrales, 1968. Group exhibitions: "Seven Photographers," University of New Mexico, Albuquerque, 1967, 1968; Westbank Gallery, Minneapolis, 1967; "Exphotage '67," Chicago, 1967; "Photography 1968," Lexington Camera Club, Lexington, Kentucky, 1968; "Young Photographers," University of New Mexico, Albuquerque, 1968; "Young Photographers '68," Purdue University, Lafayette, Indiana, 1968; Focus Gallery, San Francisco, 1968, 1969; "Light⁷," Massachusetts Institute of Technology, Cambridge, 1968. Collections: University of New Mexico Art Museum; State of New Mexico Art Museum; Massachusetts Institute of Technology. Currently Assistant Professor of Art, University of Nebraska. Address: 112 West Lakeshore, Lincoln, Nebraska 68528.

Roslyn Banish born Chicago, Illinois, 1942. Studied: Hebrew University, Jerusalem, 1961-62. Received B.A. degree in Middle Eastern Studies, University of Michigan, Ann Arbor, 1963; M.S. in Photography, Illinois Institute of Technology, 1968. Currently working as a photographer for the Mayor's Commission on Youth Welfare, Chicago, Illinois. Address: 2120 North Clark Street, Chicago, Illinois 60614.

David F. Banks born Columbus, Georgia, 1943. Received A.B. degree from Kenyon College in Art and Psychology, 1965; Jur. D. degree, University of Florida, Gainesville, 1968. Studied photography with Jerry Uelsmann. Address: 2 Grace Court, Brooklyn Heights, New York 11201.

Thomas F. Barrow born Kansas City, Missouri, 1938. Received B.F.A. degree, Kansas City Art Institute, 1963; film courses with Jack Ellis, Northwestern University, 1965; M.S. degree, Illinois Institute of Technology, 1967. Photographs published: *Student Independent VI,* Institute of Design, 1966; *Form,* No. 7 (March 1968). Group exhibitions: Riverside Studio, Rochester, New York, 1967; "Contemporary Photographers IV," traveling exhibition prepared by George Eastman House; "Photography 1968," Lexington Camera Club, Lexington, Kentucky, 1968; "Young Photographers '68," Purdue University, Lafayette, Indiana, 1968; "Light⁷," Massachusetts Institute of Technology, Cambridge, 1968; Rochester Institute of Technology, 1969. Collections: National Gallery of Canada; Museum of Modern Art, New York City; George Eastman House. Currently Assistant Curator, Research Center, George Eastman House. Address: 55 Meigs Street, Rochester, New York 14607.

David Batchelder born Titusville, Pennsylvania, 1939. Received B.A. degree, University of New Hampshire. Photographs published: *Modern Photography,* 23:11 (1959); *Aperture,* 14:1 (1968). One-man exhibitions: University of Iowa, 1967; Coe College, Cedar Rapids, 1968; Bennington College, Bennington, Vermont, 1968. Group exhibitions: Mulvane Art Center, Topeka, Kansas, 1966; Davenport Art Center, Davenport, Iowa, 1966; University of New Hampshire, Durham, 1966; Oregon State University, 1967; San Francisco State College, 1967; Western Kentucky State College, 1967; "Young Photographers '68," Purdue University, Lafayette, Indiana, 1968; "Light⁷," Massachusetts Institute of

Technology, Cambridge, 1968. Collection: Bowdoin Museum of Art, Brunswick, Maine. Currently teaching at Smith College. Address: Smith College, Department of Art, Northampton, Massachusetts 01060.

Michael Becotte born Niagara Falls, New York, 1945. Studied: Sam Houston State College, Texas. Received B.F.A. degree, Rochester Institute of Technology, 1968. Workshop with Nathan Lyons, 1966-67. Photographs published: *Symposium,* 1968. Group exhibition: Riverside Studio, Rochester, New York, 1967. Currently Head of Reproduction Center, George Eastman House. Address: 72 North Union Street, Rochester, New York 14607.

Neil Beitzell born Gill Hall, Pennsylvania, 1939. Received B.S. degree, Illinois Institute of Technology, 1962; M.F.A. degree, Rhode Island School of Design, 1964. Exhibitions: Cleveland Museum, 1965; Richmond College, 1967; Atlanta Art Festival, 1968. Address: 2112 Riverside Drive, Richmond, Virginia 23225.

Gordon Bennett born Decatur, Tennessee, 1933. Received B.A. and M.A. degrees, San Francisco State College. Studied: East Tennessee State College; Chouinard Art Institute, Los Angeles. Photographs published: *West Art* (April 1967); *Bay Guardian,* April 20, 1967; *Graphics Today* (1968). One-man exhibitions: Santa Barbara Museum of Art, 1965; San Francisco State College Library, 1965; E. B. Crocker Art Gallery, Sacramento, 1967; M. H. de Young Memorial Museum, San Francisco, 1967, Two-man exhibition: George Eastman House, 1967. Group exhibitions: "Contemporary Photographers III," traveling exhibition prepared by George Eastman House; "Photography for the Arts in the Embassies," Oakland Museum and Focus Gallery, 1967; "Photography USA," De Cordova Museum, Lincoln, Massachusetts, 1968. Collections: Museum of Modern Art, New York City; George Eastman House. Address: 427 Montford Avenue, Mill Valley, California 94941.

Michael Bishop born Palo Alto, California, 1946. Studied: Foothill College; San Francisco Art Institute; San Francisco State College. Photographs published: *San Francisco Camera,* 1:1 (1969). Group exhibition: "Photography for the Arts in the Embassies," Focus Gallery and Oakland Museum, 1967. Address: 43 Surry Street, San Francisco, California 94131.

Maureen Bisilliat born 1931. Studied painting with André Lhote, and, at the Art Students League, with Morris Kantor. Living in Brazil since 1952. One-man exhibition: São Paulo Museum of Art, 1966. Contributes articles on folklore to *Du.* Currently working on a still-animation film, a photographic interpretation of João Guimarães Rosa's book, *Grande Sertão.* Address: Rua Bela Cintra 2011, São Paulo, Brazil.

Stanley Blanchard born Rochester, New York, 1943. Received B.A. degree, University of New Hampshire, 1966; M.F.A. degree, Ohio University, Athens, Ohio, 1968. Advanced Studies Workshop, George Eastman House, 1967. One-man exhibition: University of New Hampshire, 1967. Address: 317 Oakridge Drive, Rochester, New York 14617.

Barbara Blondeau born Detroit, Michigan, 1939. Received B.F.A. degree, School of the Art Institute of Chicago; M.S. degree, Illinois Institute of Technology. Photograph published: *Photography Annual 1969.* One-man exhibitions: St. Mary's College, Notre Dame, Indiana, 1967; Northern Illinois University, De Kalb, Illinois, 1968. Group exhibitions: Illinois Institute of Technology, 1965; "FOTA," University of Chicago, 1965, 1966; "Refocus," University of Iowa, 1966; American Designers Galleries, Chicago, Illinois, 1966; Rosary College, River Forest, Illinois, 1966; St. Mary's College Faculty Show, Notre Dame, Indiana, 1967; "Chicago Area Photographers," traveling exhibition, 1968. Address: 737 South Sixth Street, Philadelphia, Pennsylvania 19147.

Donald Blumberg born New York City, 1935. Received B.S. degree, Cornell University, 1959; M.S. degree, University of Colorado, 1961. One-man exhibitions: George Eastman House, Rochester, 1966; The Jewish Center of Buffalo, Buffalo, New York, 1967. Two-man exhibition: State University of New York at Buffalo, 1966. Group exhibitions: "The 30th Annual Western New York Exhibit," Albright-Knox Art Gallery, Buffalo, 1966; Arleigh Gallery, San Francisco, 1967; "The Persistence of Vision," George Eastman House, 1967 (circulating); "Photography in the Twentieth Century," traveling exhibition prepared by George Eastman House, 1967; "The 31st Annual Western New York Exhibit," Albright-Knox Art Gallery, Buffalo, 1967; "Contemporary Photographers III," traveling exhibition prepared by George Eastman House; "Photography USA," De Cordova Museum, Lincoln, Massachusetts, 1968; Upton Gallery, Buffalo, 1968; "Contemporary Photography," University of California Art Galleries, Los Angeles, 1968; Collections: Museum of Modern Art, New York City; University of California at Los Angeles; George Eastman House. Currently Assistant Professor of Art, State University of New York at Buffalo. Address: 505 Linwood Ave., Buffalo, New York 14209.

Ladislaus Borodáč born Košice, Czechoslovakia, 1933. Studied: Higher School of Industrial Arts-Fine Arts-Photography, Bratislava. Photographs published: *Camera,* Switzerland, 1966; *Progresso Fotografico,* Italy, 1966; *Fotografie,* Czechoslovakia, 1966. Articles about: *Mladá Tvorba,* Bratislava, 1965; *Slovenské Pohlady,* Bratislava, 1965; *Creative Camera,* Number 45 (March 1968). Exhibitions: "Biennale of Youth," Paris, 1967; "Novi Sad," Yugoslavia, 1967. Collection: Galeria Mladych, Bratislava. Address: Riazanská No. 73, Bratislava, Czechoslovakia.

Dean Brown born Newport News, Virginia, 1936. Received B.A. degree, Brooklyn College, 1960; M.A. degree, New York University, 1966. Photographs published: *Photog-*

raphy Annual 1969, Oberlin Alumni Quarterly, Opera News, New York Magazine, Redbook, Fortune, Esquire. Address: 37 Walker Street, New York, New York 10013.

Robert E. Brown born Gouverneur, New York, 1937. Received B.F.A. degree, Rochester Institute of Technology, 1959; M.A. degree, San Francisco State College, 1967. Photograph published: *Aperture,* 9:4 (1961). One-man exhibitions: San Francisco State College Library, 1967; George Eastman House, 1968. Group exhibitions: Massachusetts Institute of Technology Creative Photography Gallery, 1965; Rochester Institute of Technology, 1966; Focus Gallery, San Francisco, California, 1967; Reed College, Portland, Oregon, 1968; "Young Photographers," University of New Mexico, Albuquerque, 1968; "Young Photographers '68," Purdue University, Lafayette, Indiana, 1968. Address: 18419 Napa Street, Northridge, California 91324.

Barry Burlison born Norwich, New York, 1941. Received B.S. degree in Art Education, State University of New York at Buffalo. Studied: University of Siena and Siena Art Institute, Siena, Italy, 1962; Illinois Institute of Technology, 1966-68. Photographs published: *Audit* (1964). One-man exhibition: Ritchie Gallery, Buffalo, New York, 1966. Two-man exhibition: Hull House Gallery, Chicago, 1968. Group exhibitions: Albright-Knox Art Gallery, Buffalo, 1965; Hyde Park Art Center, Chicago, 1967; University of Iowa, Iowa City, 1968; Friends of Photography Gallery, Carmel, California, 1968; Kovler Gallery, Chicago, 1968; Rosner Gallery, Chicago, 1968. Currently working as a still and motion picture photographer, Graphics Department, City of Chicago. Address: 3852 North Janssen Avenue, Chicago, Illinois 60613.

Carl Cheng born San Francisco, California, 1942. Received B.A. degree, 1963, and M.A. degree, 1967, from University of California at Los Angeles. Article about: *Artforum,* 6:7 (1968). Exhibitions: "Second Annual Small Images Show," California State College, 1967; "Plastics/1968," University of Santa Barbara, California, 1968; "Photographic Imagery—1968," San Diego State College, San Diego, California, 1968; "Young Photographers," University of New Mexico, Albuquerque, 1968; Orlando Gallery, Encino, California; Esther Robles Gallery, Los Angeles. Address: 1012 Pico, Santa Monica, California 90404.

Mark Cohen born Wilkes-Barre, Pennsylvania, 1943. Studied: Pennsylvania State University. Received B.A. degree, Wilkes College. Article about: *Leica Photography,* 18:1 (1965). One-man exhibition: Wilkes College, 1969. Currently a student at School of Visual Arts, New York City. Address: 38 North Main Street, Wilkes-Barre, Pennsylvania 18701.

David Colley born Kentucky, 1940. Received B.A. degree, Murray State University; M.A. degree, Columbia University. Photographs published: *Twelve Days at Santa Cruz,* product of workshop on the making of a photographic book, University Extension, University of California at Santa Cruz, 1967. Group exhibitions: "Young Photographers," University of New Mexico, Albuquerque, 1968; "Young Photographers '68," Purdue University, Lafayette, Indiana, 1968; University of Illinois Traveling Exhibition. Address: Farmington, Kentucky 42040.

Larry Colwell born Detroit, Michigan. Studied: Art Center School in Los Angeles; Chouinard School of Art. Photographs published: *Aperture,* 4:1 (1956), 7:1 (1959); *U. S. Camera Annual,* 1950, 1956, 1957, 1958, 1959, 1961, 1967; *American Annual of Photography 1953; Photography Today,* London, 1957; *Photography Yearbook,* London, 1958, 1960-64; *British Annual of Photography,* 1964, 1965, 1967; *Photography of the World,* Tokyo, 1958; *The World of Camera,* Lucerne, 1964; *Camera Magazine,* Lucerne, 1957; *Mobilia,* Copenhagen (February 1960); *Photography Magazine,* London (December 1964); *Fotografico,* Milan, 1957; *Asahi Magazine,* Tokyo, 1958.

One-man exhibitions: Cummer Gallery of Art, Jacksonville, Florida, 1965; Heliography Gallery, New York, 1965; Monterey County Museum of Art, Carmel, California, 1966; University of Florida, Gainesville, 1967; Jacksonville Museum of Art, Jacksonville, Florida, 1967; Gross Gallery, Eugene, Oregon, 1968; The Camera Gallery, Greenwich, Connecticut, 1968. Group exhibitions: Studio M, Jacksonville, Florida, 1965; Savannah Art Festival, Savannah, Georgia, 1967. Collections: Museum of Modern Art, New York City; M. H. de Young Memorial Museum, San Francisco; New York Public Library, New York City; Monterey County Museum of Art, Carmel, California; Jacksonville Museum of Art, Jacksonville, Florida; George Eastman House. Currently Instructor of Photography at Silvermine College of Art, New Canaan, Connecticut. Address: 41 Wolfpit Avenue, Norwalk, Connecticut 06851.

Charles Compère born Hamburg, Germany, 1935. Photographs published: *Das Deutsche Lichtbild,* 1956, 1958; *Revolution im Unsichtbaren,* 1968; *Werkung,* 1968. Two-man exhibition: "Color Safari in East Africa," Agfa Gevaert, 1966. Address: 506 Bensberg-Refrath, Jagerstr. 8, Germany.

Linda S. Connor born New York City, 1944. Received B.F.A. degree, Rhode Island School of Design. Photograph published: *Mademoiselle* (August 1966). Group exhibitions: Kovler Gallery, Chicago, 1968; Rosner Gallery, Chicago, 1968; "Refocus," University of Iowa, 1968. Collections: Art Institute of Chicago; George Eastman House. Currently graduate student at Illinois Institute of Technology. Address: 367 Cedar Lane, New Canaan, Conn. 06840.

Pierre Cordier born Brussels, Belgium, 1933. Studied Political Science at the University of Brussels; studied Photography with Otto Steinert. Articles about: *Les Beaux Arts,* No. 836 (December 1958); *L'Arc,* No. 21 (Spring 1963); *Photo-Tribune* (February 1964); *Terre d'Images,* No. 8 (July 1965); *Popular Photography Italiana,*

No. 110 (August 1966). Group exhibitions: "Salon Comparaisons," Paris, 1965; "Photo-graphie," 1966, 1967; "Galerie les Contards," Lacoste, 1966; "Artek Gallery," Helsinki, 1967; Museum of Modern Art, New York City, 1967; "Generative Fotografie," Bielefeld, Germany, 1968. Collections: Board of Culture and National Education, Belgium; Museum of Modern Art, New York City. Address: 22 Avenue Solvay, La Hulpe, Belgium.

Thomas Cugini born Zurich, Switzerland, 1938. Studied: Arts and Crafts School, Zurich. Photographs published: *Du; Capital; Asahi Camera; Photographis 1967, 1968; Camera.* Exhibitions: "Viva Mexico," Zurich, 1967; "Viva Mexico," Cologne, 1968. Address: Dolderstrasse 2, 8032 Zurich, Switzerland.

Darryl J. Curran born California, 1935. Studied: Ventura College. Received B.A. degree, 1960, and M.A. degree, 1964, from University of California at Los Angeles. Group exhibitions: Canyon Gallery, Topanga Canyon, 1965, 1967; "Photography 1968," San Diego State College, 1968; "Young Photographers '68," Purdue University, Lafayette, Indiana, 1968; Los Angeles Harbor College, 1968; "Art Unlimited," Downey Art Museum, 1968. Address: 2139 South Bentley Avenue, Los Angeles, California 90025.

Robert D'Alessandro born New York City, 1942. Received B.F.A. degree, Pratt Institute, 1965. Peace Corps volunteer to Brazil, 1965. Exhibition: "Artesanato Do Nordeste," University of Paraiba, 1967. Currently teaching art at Levittown High School. Address: 131 Willoughby Avenue, Brooklyn, New York 11205.

Judy Dater born Los Angeles, California, 1941. Received B.A. degree, 1963, and M.A. degree, 1966, San Francisco State College. Studied: University of California at Los Angeles. Published: *Aperture,* 14:1 (1968). One-man show: Aardvark Gallery, San Francisco, 1965. Group exhibitions:

Loren Gallery, San Francisco, 1965, "Urban Reality," traveling exhibition sponsored by SPUR of San Francisco, 1966; University of Oregon, 1967; "Photography in the Fine Arts V," 1967; "Photography USA," De Cordova Museum, Lincoln, Massachusetts, 1968; "Light⁷," Massachusetts Institute of Technology, Cambridge, 1968. Collections: Kinsey Institute, University of Indiana; Massachusetts Institute of Technology. Address: 33 Houston Street, San Francisco, California 94133.

Donald Dickinson born Bronxville, New York, 1941. Received B.F.A. degree, 1965, and M.F.A. degree, 1968, Rochester Institute of Technology. Studied: University of California at Santa Barbara, 1964. Workshops with Minor White, 1963; with Nathan Lyons, 1963-64, 1965-66. One-man exhibitions: IBM Research Center, Yorktown, New York, 1966; Rochester Institute of Technology, 1966. Group exhibitions: Riverside Studio, Rochester, New York, 1965, 1967. Currently on faculty of Ryerson Polytechnical Institute, Toronto, Ontario. Address: House No. 23, 1560 Bloor Street, Mississauga, Ontario, Canada.

Clyde Dilley born Modesto, California, 1939. Received B.A. degree, 1967, and M.A. degree, 1968, from San Francisco State College. Group exhibitions: San Francisco Bay Area Urban Renewal League Traveling Exhibition, 1966; University of Santa Clara, 1967; University of New Mexico, 1968; "Refocus," University of Iowa, 1968. Collection: University of Santa Clara. Currently teaching photography at San Jacinto College. Address: San Jacinto College, 8060 Spencer Highway, Pasadena, Texas 77505.

Ellen Epstein born Rochester, New York, 1943. Received B.A. degree, 1965, and M.A. degree, 1968, from University of Iowa. One-man exhibitions: Civic Center, Iowa City, Iowa, 1966; Gallery for the Advancement of Photography, Iowa City, 1967; First National Bank, Iowa City, 1967. Two-man exhibition: Stephens College, Columbia,

Missouri, 1966. Group exhibitions: University of New Hampshire, Durham, 1966; Dartmouth College, 1966; Cinemation Studio, Iowa City, Iowa, 1966, 1967; Davenport Art Center, Davenport, Iowa, 1966; University of Western Kentucky, 1967; San Francisco State College, 1967; Oregon State University, 1967; Iowa Memorial Union, Iowa City, 1968; "Young Photographers," University of New Mexico, Albuquerque, 1968. Address: 245 South Riverside Court, Iowa City, Iowa 52240.

Kurt W. Erben born Vienna, Austria, 1946. Studied with Otto Steinert at Folkwangschule für Gestaltung; at Fachschule für Fotografie an der Höheren Grafishen Lehr- und Versuchsanstalt, Vienna, Austria. Article published with Hans Peter Klemenz, "The Hour before the Bullfight," *Camera,* 46:6 (1967). Collection: Höhere Grafische Lehr- und Versuchsanstalt, Vienna, Austria. Address: Linzer Strasse 147-6, A-1140, Vienna 14, Austria.

Donald J. Erceg born Portland, Oregon, 1939. Received B.A. degree, 1961. Studied photography with Minor White. Photograph published: *Aperture,* 14:1 (1968). Group exhibitions: Massachusetts Institute of Technology, 1965; "5 Photographers," Orange Coast College, 1966; "Art Annual," University of Oregon, 1966; "Interim 66," Portland, Oregon, 1966; "Light⁷," Massachusetts Institute of Technology, 1968. Address: 481 Cambridge Street, Cambridge, Massachusetts 02141.

Jiři Erml born Brno, Czechoslovakia, 1945. Photographs published: *Kulturni Tvorba, Mlady Svet, Foto-Film.* Currently completing studies in the department of Art Photography at Prague's Film and Television Academy. Address: Ondrickova 31, Prague 3, Czechoslovakia.

James Fallon born Malone, New York, 1946. Received B.F.A. degree, Rochester Institute of Technology, 1968. Group exhibition: "Photography as Printmaking," Museum of Modern Art, New York City,

1968. Collection: Museum of Modern Art, New York City. Address: c/o Mr. F. Fallon, 48 Marlboro Rd., Delmar, New York 12054.

Antonio A. Fernandez born Havana, Cuba, 1941. Received B.A. degree in Political Science, University of Florida, Gainesville, 1963. Peace Corps Volunteer to Panama, 1964-66. Currently graduate student at Illinois Institute of Technology. Address: 160 SW 52nd Court, Miami, Florida 33134.

Benedict J. Fernandez born New York City 1935. Attended Columbia University; studied photography with Alexis Brodovitch, Minor White, Richard Avedon, and Marvin Israel. Working as free-lance photographer in New York City since 1960. Photographs published: Cover of *New York Times Magazine,* June 5, 1966; numerous photographs in *New York Times Magazine* and other newspapers; biographical sketch with photographs in *Noël Noël Alumni,* Parsons School of Design, 1966-67; contributing photographer to *Pacifica Radio Program Folio; Dissent,* 1967, CBC Canada; *Conscience for Change, Martin Luther King, Jr., Massey Lectures,* 1967, CBC Canada; *Medical World News* (September 1967); *I Have a Dream, Time/Life,* 1968; *In Opposition: Images of American Dissent in the Sixties* (Da Capo, 1968). One-man exhibitions: Parsons School of Design, New York City, 1966; James Weldon Johnson Theater Arts Center, 1966; Brooklyn Academy of Music, New York City, 1967; "Little Red School House," New York City, 1967; "School Art League," New York City, 1967; Civil Liberties Union (circulating exhibition); Brooklyn Children's Museum, New York, 1968; Shakespeare Festival, New York City, 1968; Parsons School of Design, New York, 1968; "Photography/Cinematography," Roxbury, Massachusetts, 1968; "Conscience," George Eastman House, 1968 (circulating exhibition). Currently Instructor of Photography, Parsons School of Design; Director of Photography, Brooklyn Children's Museum; Member of Steering Committee of ASMP Design Laboratory. Address: 1433 37th St., North Bergen, New Jersey 07047.

Carl Fleischhauer born Columbus, Ohio, 1940. Received B.A. degree, Kenyon College, 1962; majored in Philosophy. Received Fulbright Grant to India, 1962-63. Currently M.F.A. candidate at Ohio University. Address: Route 5, Athens, Ohio 45701.

Steven D. Foster born Piqua, Ohio, 1945. Received B.S. degree, Illinois Institute of Technology. Workshop with Nathan Lyons, 1964-66. Group exhibitions: Underground Gallery, New York City, 1967; Friends of Photography Gallery, Carmel, California, 1968. Address: 1 Bank Street, Apartment 4-A, New York, New York 10014.

Jill Freedman self-taught as a photographer. Photograph published: *Photography Annual 1969, Life.* Exhibition: "Four Points of View on Resurrection City," Brooklyn Children's Museum, New York, 1968. Address: 181 Sullivan Street, Brooklyn, New York 11231.

Chuck Fridenmaker born Phoenix, Arizona, 1940. Received B.F.A. degree, Arizona State University. Group exhibitions: "Young Photographers '68," Purdue University, Lafayette, Indiana, 1968; "Refocus," University of Iowa, 1968; "Yuma Fine Arts Association Invitational Exhibit," Arizona, 1968. Currently graduate student at Arizona State University. Address: 534 East Huntington Drive, Apartment 6, Tempe, Arizona 85281.

Oliver L. Gagliani born Placerville, California, 1917. Studied: San Francisco State College, 1940-42; Heald's College, 1951-54. Workshops with Ansel Adams, Minor White, Ruth Bernhard. Photograph published: *Aperture,* 14:1 (1968). Exhibitions: South San Francisco Public Library, 1965; San Francisco State College, 1967; "Photography for the Art in the Embassies," Focus Gallery and Oakland Museum, 1967; Focus Gallery, 1968; "Light⁷," Massachusetts Institute of Technology, Cambridge, 1968. Address: 605 Rocca Avenue, South San Francisco, California 94080.

Richard Gates born Kettering, England, 1943. Studied: Hereford Cathedral School. Address: 5 Dalkieth Avenue, Kettering, England.

William Gedney born Albany, New York, 1932. One-man exhibition: Museum of Modern Art, New York City, 1968. Group exhibition: "Photography in the Twentieth Century," traveling exhibition prepared by George Eastman House, 1967. Received Guggenheim Fellowship, 1966-67. Collections: Museum of Modern Art, New York City; George Eastman House. Address: 467 Myrtle Ave., Brooklyn, New York 11205.

Elly Gordon born Boston, Massachusetts, 1943. Received B.F.A. degree, Boston University; M.F.A. Pratt Institute. Address: 292 Clinton Avenue, Brooklyn, New York 11205.

Emmett Gowin II born Danville, Virginia, 1941. Received B.F.A. degree, Richmond Professional Institute, 1965; M.F.A. degree, Rhode Island School of Design, 1967. One-man exhibitions: Dayton Art Institute, 1968; Illinois Institute of Technology, 1968; University of Richmond, 1968. Group exhibition: "Young Photographers '68," Purdue University, Lafayette, Indiana, 1968. Collection: Museum of Modern Art, New York City. Currently teaching photography at the School of the Dayton Art Institute, Dayton, Ohio. Address: 138 Edgewood Avenue, Dayton, Ohio 45407.

Betty Hahn born Chicago, Illinois, 1940. Received A.B. degree, 1963, and M.F.A. degree, 1966, from Indiana University. Workshop with Nathan Lyons, 1967-68. Group exhibitions: "Contemporary Photography Since 1950," traveling exhibition prepared by George Eastman House; "Photography in the Twentieth Century," traveling exhibition prepared by George Eastman House, 1967. Collection: George Eastman House. Address: 281 Mt. Vernon Avenue, Rochester, New York 14620.

Robert F. Haiko born Hartford, Connecticut, 1942. Received B.F.A. degree, Boston University, 1965; M.F.A. degree, Rhode Island School of Design, 1968. Workshop with Minor White, 1965; Advanced Studies Workshop, George Eastman House, 1967. Photographs published: "Portfolio RISD," 1967; *Boston Review of Photography*, No. 4 (January 1968). Group exhibitions: "The Other Side," Massachusetts Institute of Technology, Cambridge, 1966; Massachusetts College of Art, 1966; Maryland Institute College of Art, 1966; Roger Williams Community Center, 1967. Address: 37 Sharon Lane, Wethersfield, Conn. 06109.

Zdeněk Halámek born Plzeň, Czechoslovakia, 1943. Studied: Building Technical School. Photographs published in Czech newspapers and journals. Group exhibitions: "Youth," Czechoslovak National Exhibit, 1967; "50 Years of ČSR," Czechoslovak National Exhibit, 1968; "Man and Time," Czechoslovak National Exhibit, 1968; "Premfoto," Přelouč, 1968. Address: Výhledy 90, Holýšov u Plzne, Czechoslovakia.

Chauncey Hare born 1934. Received B.A. and B.S. degrees, Columbia University, 1955 and 1956. One-man exhibitions: "Hills of California," San Francisco Museum of Art, 1966; "Utah and the Four Corners," M. H. de Young Memorial Museum, 1968. Collections: Oakland Museum; Museum of Modern Art, New York City. Address: 287 Kenyon Ave., Berkeley, California 94708.

Pamela Harris-McLeod born Erie, Pennsylvania, 1942. Received B.A. in English Literature from Pomona College, Claremont, California. Studied photography with Stephen Gersh, 1966. Collection: National Film Board of Canada. Address: 318 Glen Road, Toronto, Canada.

Robert Häusser born Stuttgart, Germany. Photographs published: *Ein Fotograf sicht Mannheim*, Bibliographisches Institut Mannheim, 1957; *Foto-Prisma*, Düsseldorf, 1958, 1960; *Das Deutsche Lichtbild*, Stuttgart, 1959; Heidelberg (Thorbeke Konstanz, 1961); *Welt am Oberrhein* (Braun, 1961-63); *Das Elsass* (Braun Karlsruhe, 1962); *Aus unseren Fenstern* (Stromeyer AG, 1962); *Fetisch des Jahrhunderts* (Vienna and Düsseldorf, 1964); *Problematik des Jurierens* (Aufsatz, 1967). Group exhibitions: "Magischer Realismus," Europhot, Switzerland, 1967; "Weltausstellung der Photographie," 1968. Collection: Museum of Modern Art, New York City. Address: 68 Mannheim, Ladenburgerstrasse 23, Germany.

R. Eugene Hayes born Attica, Indiana, 1936. Received B.A. degree, Southern Illinois University, 1965. Group exhibitions: Gallery Creativity, Southern Illinois University, 1965; Illinois Institute of Technology, 1966; "Refocus," University of Iowa, 1967; "Young Photographers," University of New Mexico, Albuquerque, 1968; "Photography 1968," Lexington Camera Club, Lexington, Kentucky, 1968. Currently graduate student at Indiana University. Address: No. 802 Redbud Hill, Bloomington, Indiana 47401.

Robert F. Heinecken born Denver, Colorado, 1931. Received B.A. and M.A. degrees, University of California at Los Angeles. Photographs published: *Artforum* (February 1968); *Photo Imagination*, by Robert Niece, 1967; "Photographs for Collectors," *Art in America* (January/February 1968); *Camera*, Switzerland, (January 1968). One-man exhibitions: California State College, Los Angeles, 1966; Mills College, 1966; Focus Gallery, San Francisco, 1968. Group exhibitions: "American Photography: The Sixties," University of Nebraska, 1966; "Professors of Photography," University of California at Los Angeles, 1966; "Contemporary Photography Since 1950," traveling exhibition prepared by George Eastman House, 1966; "Projected Art," Finch College Museum, New York City, 1967; "Photographs for Collectors," Museum of Modern Art, New York City, 1967; "Photography in the Twentieth Century," traveling exhibition prepared by George Eastman House, 1967; "Persistence of Vision," George Eastman House, 1967 (circulating); "Photography as Printmaking," Museum of Modern Art, New York City, 1968; "Photographic Imagery/1968," San Diego State College Art Gallery, 1968; "Photography USA," De Cordova Museum, Lincoln, Massachusetts, 1968. Collections: Museum of Modern Art, New York City; George Eastman House; Mills College Art Gallery; Oakland Museum of Art, Oakland, California. Currently Assistant Professor of Art at University of California at Los Angeles. Address: 10300 Viretta Lane, Los Angeles, California 90024.

Reginald Heron born Marseille, France, 1932. Received B.S. degree, 1963, and M.S. degree, 1966, from Illinois Institute of Technology. Taught photography at Institute of Design, 1963-66. Photographs published: *London* (private printing, 1961), *Good Photography*, Vol. 12 (April 1956); *Student Independent V*, Institute of Design, 1965; *Form*, No. 7 (March 1968). One-man exhibitions: State Historical Society of Wisconsin, 1966; Rochester Public Library, 1967; Aquinas Institute, 1967. Group exhibitions: Traveling exhibition prepared by the Institute of Design, 1967; New York State University at New Paltz, 1967; Riverside Studio, Rochester, New York, 1967; "Photography 1968," Lexington Camera Club, Lexington, Kentucky, 1968; "Contemporary Photographers IV," traveling exhibition prepared by George Eastman House. Collections: George Eastman House; Art Institute of Chicago; State Historical Society of Wisconsin; National Gallery of Canada. Currently Assistant Curator, Equipment Archive, George Eastman House. Address: 1845 East Avenue, Rochester, New York 14610.

Warren M. Hill born Melrose, Massachusetts, 1928. Self-taught as a photographer. Photograph published: *Boston Review of Photography* (March 1968). Group exhibitions: "12 Photographers of the American Social Landscape," Brandeis University, 1967; "Young Photographers '68," Purdue University, Lafayette, Indiana, 1968; "Photography USA," De Cordova Museum, Lincoln, Massachusetts, 1968; "Photographs from the Carl Siembab Gallery," originated by the Minneapolis Institute of Art, 1969. Address: 799 Cambridge Street, Cambridge, Massachusetts 02141.

Bradley Hindson born Erie, Pennsylvania, 1935. Received B.A. degree, Rutgers University, 1957; M.F.A. degree, Ohio University, 1964. Article about: *The New York Times,* December 5, 1965. Exhibitions: Underground Gallery, New York City, 1965; Memorial Art Gallery, Rochester, 1966; Rochester Institute of Technology, 1967. Currently Assistant Professor of Photography at Rochester Institute of Technology. Address: Gilbert Mill Road, Honeoye Falls, New York 14472.

Walter Hirsch born Sweden, 1935. Photographs published: *Swedish Photographic Yearbook* 1965-68; *Popular Fotografi* (February 1967). One-man exhibition: Museum of Modern Art, Stockholm, 1968. Group exhibitions: "Young Photographers," Museum of Modern Art, Stockholm, 1966, 1967, 1968; Milano Triennial, 1968. Collection: The Swedish Photographic Museum. Address: Skillinggränd 7, Stockholm, Sweden 11220.

Hisae Imai Photographs published: *Energy,* 3:3 (1966), 4:1 (1967), 5:1 (1968), 5:2 (1968); *CamerArt,* 11:5 (September/October 1968). Address: 1-6-9 Kita Koenji Suginami-ku, Tokyo, Japan.

Brian M. Jacobs born Ohio, 1943. Received B.A. degree, California State College at Los Angeles. Address: 602 Durwood Drive, La Canada, California 91011.

Håkan Johansson born Borås, Sweden, 1939. Studied photography with Otto Steinert at the Folkwangschule für Gestaltung, Essen, Germany. Photographs published: *Du Atlantis,* Switzerland, 1964; *Populär Fotografi,* 1967-68; *Das Deutsche Lichtbild* 1965-69. Group exhibitions: "Otto Steinert und Schüler," Folkwangmuseum Essen, 1967; Oberhausen, 1968; "Die Brucke,"

Düsseldorf, 1968. Address: 4 Düsseldorf-Oberkassel, Lueg-Allee 4, West Germany.

Harold H. Jones III born Morristown, New Jersey, 1940. Received B.F.A. degree, Maryland Institute, 1965; candidate for M.F.A. degree, University of New Mexico, Albuquerque. Awarded George Eastman House Work-Study Fellowship, 1967. One-man exhibitions: Cinema East, Baltimore, Maryland, 1965; University of California at Davis, 1969. Two-man exhibitions: Sandia Base Art Center, Albuquerque, 1967; Quivera Gallery, Corrales, New Mexico, 1967. Group exhibitions: University of Kentucky, 1965; "Seven Photographers," Jonson Gallery, Albuquerque, 1967, 1968; West Bank Gallery, Minneapolis, Minnesota, 1967; "Exphotage," Chicago, 1967; "Young Photographers," University of New Mexico, Albuquerque, 1968; "Photography 1968," Lexington Camera Club, Lexington, Kentucky, 1968; Friends of Photography Gallery, Carmel, California, 1968; San Francisco State College, 1968; Focus Gallery, San Francisco, 1968, 1969; "Young Photographers '68," Purdue University, Lafayette, Indiana, 1968; Rochester Institute of Technology, 1969. Currently Assistant Curator, Exhibitions, George Eastman House. Address: 18 Vick Park B, Rochester, New York 14607.

Jo Diane Kasper born Dubuque, Iowa, 1945. Received B.F.A. degree, Arizona State University. Studied photography with Jack Stuler, David Allen Kent, John Schulze. Currently graduate student in Education at University of Iowa. Address: 11823 North 22nd Street, Phoenix, Arizona 85028.

Bruce Katsiff born Philadelphia, Pennsylvania, 1945. Received B.F.A. degree, Rochester Institute of Technology. Studied: Pennsylvania State College; Philadelphia College of Art. Currently teaching photography at Bucks County Community College. Address: Lumberville, Pennsylvania 18933.

Kikuji Kawada born Ibaragi, Japan, 1933. Studied: St. Paul's University, Tokyo, 1955; majored in Economics. Photographs published: *The Map* (Bijutsu Shuppan-sha, Tokyo, 1965). Exhibition: "The Fantastic World," Nikon Camera Gallery, Tokyo, 1968. Address: 3-8 Sadowaracho, Shinjukuku, Tokyo.

Dennis C. Kievets born Cleveland, Ohio, 1937. Received B.F.A. degree, 1959, and M.A. degree, 1961, from Kent State University. Workshops with Minor White. One-man exhibition: Hiram College, 1968. Group exhibitions: Massachusetts Institute of Technology Group Show, 1965; G. A. R. Hall, Peninsula, 1966. Address: 7912 Middlesex Road, Mentor, Ohio 44060.

Rosalind S. Kimball born Buffalo, New York, 1941. Studied: State University of New York at Buffalo; Goethe Institute, Passau, Germany. Peace Corps volunteer to India, 1964-65. Studied photography with Minor White. Photograph published: *Aperture,* 14:1 (1968). Group exhibition: "Light[7]," Massachusetts Institute of Technology, Cambridge, 1968. Address: c/o Mrs. Stockton Kimball, 215 South Cayuga Road, Williamsville, New York 14221.

Irwin B. Klein born Brooklyn, New York, 1933. Received B.A. degree, Queens College, 1955; M.A. degree, University of Chicago, 1956; majored in English. Article about: *Modern Photography,* 28:8 (1964). Group exhibitions: "Recent Acquisitions," Museum of Modern Art, New York City, 1966; "The Photographer's Forum," Institutio Mexicano Norteamericano Relationes Culturales, 1966; "The People Protest," Columbia University, 1967. Collection: Museum of Modern Art, New York City. Address: 189 East Seventh Street, New York, New York 10009.

Jim Kraft born Evanston, Illinois, 1938. Received B.A. degree, University of Arkansas. Photograph published: *Photography Annual 1968.* Group exhibitions: "Photography 1968," Lexington Camera Club, Lexington, Kentucky, 1968; "Young Photographers," University of New Mexico, Albuquerque, 1968; "Young Photographers '68," Purdue University, Lafayette, Indiana, 1968; Friends of Photography Gallery, Carmel, California, 1968; "New Mexico Photographers," Santa Fe, 1968; "Seven Photographers," University of New Mexico, Albuquerque, 1968; Focus Gallery, San Francisco, 1969. Currently M.F.A. candidate at University of New Mexico. Address: 1221 Columbia Drive, NE, Albuquerque, New Mexico 87106.

Arthur Kramer born New York City, 1924. Studied photography with Berenice Abbott. Began working as a photojournalist, 1935 until 1955; interrupted by service as a Photo-officer in the Air Force in World War II. Was a member of the Association of Heliographers, with exhibitions at the Heliography Gallery, Lever House, Van Ness Galleries, Village Camera Club, New York Camera Club. Two-man exhibition: George Eastman House, 1968. He has contributed numerous articles and photographs to *Modern Photography, Popular Photography, U.S. Camera, Photography* (Sweden), *Asahi Camera.* Currently Contributing Editor to Modern Photography and a Vice-President at J. Walter Thompson, New York City. Address: 29 Laura Drive, Westbury, New York 11590.

Leslie R. Krims born Brooklyn, New York, 1943. Received B.F.A. degree, Cooper Union; M.F.A. degree, Pratt Institute, 1966. Portfolio published: *Aperture,* 13:3 (1967). Currently Instructor of Photography, Rochester Institute of Technology. Address: 167 State Street, Rochester, New York 14614.

Paul Krot born Brooklyn, New York, 1939. Received B.S. degree, State University of New York at Buffalo, 1962; M.F.A. Rhode Island School of Design, 1968. Photograph published: *Boston Review of Photography,* No. 4 (1968). Group exhibitions: "Portfolio '67," Photo Society, Rhode Island School of Design; Museum of Fine Arts, Providence, 1968; Rhode Island Arts Festival, 1968. Currently Instructor of Photog-

raphy at Rhode Island School of Design. Address: 411 Atwells Avenue, Providence, Rhode Island 02909.

Kunié born 1942. Studied: Ochanomizu University, Japan; majored in Physics. Received B.F.A. degree, School of the Art Institute of Chicago. Articles about: *Modern Photography,* 32:2 (1968); *U. S. Camera,* 31:11 (1968). Address: 908 Amsterdam Avenue, New York, New York 10025.

Tatsuo Kurihara born Tokyo, Japan, 1937. Graduated from School of Economics and Politics of Waseda University, Tokyo, 1961. Photographs published: *Asahi Camera Annual,* 1961, 1967; *Asahi Camera* (March, May, August, and December 1968); *Camera Mainichi* (September, 1968); *Photo Art* (September 1968), and other publications. One-man exhibition: "Europe — Post-war Years," Tokyo, 1968. Group Exhibitions: "Press Photographers Exhibit," Tokyo, 1965, 1966, 1967. Collection: Museum of Modern Art, Tokyo. Address: c/o Ito Shoes Building 3F, 3-3 Kyobashi Chuo-ku, Tokyo, Japan.

William G. Larson born North Tonawanda, New York, 1942. Received B.S. degree, State University of New York at Buffalo; M.S. degree, Illinois Institute of Technology. Studied: University of Siena. Photographs published: *Modern Photography,* 31:9 (1967); *Photography Annual 1968.* Group exhibitions: State University of New York at Buffalo, 1966; "FOTA," University of Chicago, 1966; "Graduate Photography," Purdue University, Lafayette, Indiana, 1966; Twentieth Century Gallery, Williamsburg, Virginia, 1966; "Bytown International Exhibition," Ottawa, Canada, 1967; "Young Photographers," University of New Mexico, Albuquerque, 1968; "Personal Images," N. W. Ayer Gallery, Washington Square, Philadelphia, Pennsylvania, 1968; Friends of Photography Gallery, Carmel, California, 1968. Currently teaching photography at Temple University. Address: 415 East Church Road, Elkins Park, Pennsylvania 19117.

Nick Lawrence born New York City, 1940. Received B.A. degree, Cornell University, 1962. Studied photography with Lisette Model at the New School for Social Research, 1967. Photographs published: *Step by Step* (Norton, 1965). Address: 172 Stanton Street, New York, New York 10002.

Robert Lebeck born Berlin, Germany, 1929. Became actively interested in photography, 1953. Photographs published: *Leica Fotografie,* No. 3 (1963); *Photography Year Book,* 1967; *U. S. Camera Annual,* 1968; *Photography Annual* 1968, 1969; in German photography annuals since 1958. One-man traveling exhibition: "Tokio, Moscow, Leopoldville," exhibited in ten major cities in Germany, 1963-65. Currently working for *Stern* magazine. Address: 2 Hamburg 13, St. Benedict Street 34, Hamburg, Germany.

James Lemkin born New Haven, Connecticut, 1946. Received B.A. degree, University of Rochester, 1968. Workshop with William B. Giles, 1965-67; with Nathan Lyons, 1966-67. Photographs published: *Scope,* 1966; *Prologue,* 1965-68; *Aperture,* 14:1 (1968). One-man exhibition: "Urban Photographs," University of Rochester, 1968. Group exhibition: "Light[7]," Massachusetts Institute of Technology, Cambridge, Massachusetts, 1968. Address: 270 Knollwood Drive, New Haven, Connecticut 06515.

Joanne Leonard born Los Angeles, California, 1940. Received B.A. degree in Social Science, University of California, 1962; graduate studies in Photography and Anthropology, San Francisco State College. Workshop with Minor White. Photographs published: *Visual Anthropology* (Holt, Rinehart & Winston, 1967). Article about: *Artforum,* 6:8 (1968). One-man exhibition: "Our Town," M. H. de Young Memorial Museum, San Francisco, 1968. Group exhibitions: "San Francisco Women Artists' Annual," San Francisco Museum, 1966; "Photography for the Art in the Embassies," Focus Gallery and Oakland Art Museum, 1967; Focus Gallery, San Francisco, 1968. Collection: Oakland Art Museum. Address: 322 Lewis Street, Oakland, California 94607.

Jacquelin Livingston born Phoenix, Arizona, 1943. Received B.A. and M.A. degrees, Arizona State University, 1964 and 1966; majored in Education. Studied: San Francisco State College. Group exhibitions: "Arizona Photographic Annual," Phoenix Art Museum, 1967; "Young Photographers," University of New Mexico, Albuquerque, 1968. Address: 3868 22nd Street, San Francisco, California 94114.

Rocco M. Lodise born Jackson, Michigan, 1941. Received B.S. degree, University of Michigan, 1965. One-man exhibition: "de nuevo arte 1967," American Cultural Center Galleries in Managua, Nicaragua. Group exhibition: Biennial Michiana Regional, 1968. Currently a graduate student at University of Michigan. Address: 1030 Arbordale, Apartment 12, Ann Arbor, Michigan 48104.

Ronald L. MacNeil born Wichita, Kansas, 1941. Studied photography with Minor White. Photographs published: *Boston Review of Photography*, No. 3 (1967); *Aperture*, 14:1 (1968). Group exhibition: "Light⁷," Massachusetts Institute of Technology, Cambridge, 1968. Address: 117 Walden Street, Cambridge, Mass. 02140.

Alen MacWeeney born Dublin, Ireland, 1939. Studied: Private schools in Dublin, until 1956; with Richard Avedon. Photographs published in numerous periodicals including: *Harper's Bazaar* (December 1965); *Idea and Image* (1967); *U. S. Camera* (April 1967); *Creative Camera* (December 1968). Exhibitions: Focus Gallery, 1968; "Light⁷," Massachusetts Institute of Technology, Cambridge, 1968. Collection: Museum of Modern Art, New York City. Address: 709 Riverside Drive, New York, New York 10032.

Jerald C. Maddox born Decatur, Indiana, 1933. Received A.B. degree, 1955, and M.A. degree, 1960, from Indiana State University. Workshop with Minor White, 1965. Published: Introduction to exhibition catalog, *American Photography: The Sixties* (University of Nebraska, 1966). Address: 4514 Highland Avenue, Bethesda, Maryland 20014.

Mary Ellen Mark born Philadelphia, Pennsylvania, 1941. Received B.F.A. degree, University of Pennsylvania, 1962; M.A. in Communication, Annenberg School of Communication, 1964. Fulbright Scholarship to Turkey, 1965-66. Photographs published: *U. S. Camera Annual,* 1966, 1968; *Modern Photography; Infinity; Look; Leica; Evergreen Review.* Exhibitions: Greer Gallery, New York City, 1966; U.S.I.A. Gallery, Istanbul, Turkey, 1967. Address: 67 Park Avenue, New York, New York 10016.

Michael McLoughlin born Peoria, Illinois, 1936. Received B.F.A. degree, Pratt Institute, 1963. Studied: Alexis Brodovitch's Design Laboratory, 1963; Advanced Studies Workshop, George Eastman House, 1967. One-man exhibitions: Doane College, Crete, Nebraska, 1966; Sheldon Memorial Art Gallery, Lincoln, Nebraska, 1967; University of Oregon, Eugene, 1968; Focus Gallery, San Francisco, 1968. Group exhibitions: Museum of Modern Art, 1965; "American Photography: The Sixties," Sheldon Memorial Art Gallery, 1966; "Professors of Photography: A National Exhibit," Association of Western Art Museums, 1966-67; "Photography USA," De Cordova Museum, Lincoln, Massachusetts, 1968. Collections: Museum of Modern Art, New York City; Sheldon Memorial Art Gallery. Address: Department of Art, University of Connecticut, Storrs, Connecticut 06268.

Larry McPherson born Newark, Ohio, 1943. Studied: Ohio State University; Rochester Institute of Technology. Photographs published: *Symposium,* 1967. Address: 4536 North Wolcott Ave., Chicago, Illinois 60640.

Roger Mertin born Bridgeport, Connecticut, 1942. Received B.F.A. degree, Rochester Institute of Technology, 1965. Workshop with Minor White, 1963; with Nathan Lyons, 1963-64, 1965-66. Photographs published: *Form,* No. 7 (March 1968). One-man exhibitions: Rochester Institute of Technology, 1965; George Eastman House, 1966. Group exhibitions: "Photography '65," New York State Exposition, 1965; Riverside Studio, Rochester, 1965, 1967; School of the Art Institute of Chicago, 1966; Illinois Institute of Technology, 1966; "Contemporary Photography Since 1950," traveling exhibition prepared by George Eastman House, 1967; "Photography in the Twentieth Century," traveling exhibition prepared by George Eastman House; Westbank Gallery, Minneapolis, 1967; The Underground Gallery, New York City, 1967; "Contemporary Photographers IV," traveling exhibition prepared by George Eastman House; "Photography 1968," Lexington Camera Club, Lexington, Kentucky, 1968; "Photography USA," De Cordova Museum, Lincoln, Massachusetts, 1968; "Light⁷," Massachusetts Institute of Technology, 1968; Rochester Institute of Technology, 1969. Collections: George Eastman House; National Gallery of Canada. Currently Assistant Curator, Extension Activities, George Eastman House. Address: 33 Goodman Street South, Rochester, New York 14607.

Ronald Mesaros born Rahway, New Jersey, 1942. Received B.F.A. degree, Rochester Institute of Technology; M.S. degree, Illinois Institute of Technology. Workshop with Minor White, 1963; with Nathan Lyons, 1964-65. Group exhibitions: "The Farmer Today," Rochester Institute of Technology, 1965; Art Directors Club of Chicago, 1967. Address: 2614 West 7th Street, Los Angeles, California 90057.

Gary Metz born Detroit, Michigan, 1941. Studied: Cleveland Institute of Art; Oberlin College. Received B.F.A. degree, Rochester Institute of Technology, 1968. Workshop with Nathan Lyons. Group exhibitions: Cleveland May Show, 1966; Riverside Studio, Rochester, 1968; "Photography as Printmaking," Museum of Modern

Art, New York City, 1968. Collections: Memorial Art Gallery, Rochester; Museum of Modern Art, New York City; National Gallery of Canada; George Eastman House. Awarded Internship in Photography, Museum of Modern Art, New York City, 1968-69. Address: c/o Department of Photography, Museum of Modern Art, 11 West 53rd Street, New York, New York 10022.

Joel Meyerowitz born New York City, 1938. Received B.F.A. degree, Ohio State University, 1959. Photographs published: *Infinity* (April 1966); *Art Voices* (July 1966); *Form*, No. 7 (March 1968). One-man exhibitions: Underground Gallery, New York City, 1966; George Eastman House, 1966. Group exhibitions: "Photography in the Twentieth Century," traveling exhibition prepared by George Eastman House, 1967; "Contemporary Photographers III," traveling exhibition prepared by George Eastman House. Collection: George Eastman House. Address: 817 West End Avenue, New York, New York 10025.

Chester J. Michalik born Holyoke, Massachusetts, 1935. Received B.S. degree, Massachusetts College of Art; M.F.A. degree, Boston University. Fulbright Fellowship to Poland for Film and Photography, 1967. One-man exhibition: Carl Siembab Gallery, Boston, 1967. Group exhibitions: University of New Hampshire, 1965; Cosindas Gallery, 1965; Gallery 216, New York City, 1965; Massachusetts Institute of Technology, Cambridge, 1965; Carl Siembab Gallery, Boston, 1967; "Young Photographers," Purdue University, Lafayette, Indiana, 1968; Rhode Island School of Design Museum, 1968; Worcester Art Museum, Worcester, Massachusetts, 1968; Rhode Island Arts Festival, 1968; "Photographs from the Siembab Gallery," originated by the Minneapolis Institute of Art, 1969. Collection: Worcester Art Museum. Address: 6 Walley St., Bristol, R. I. 02809.

Duane Michals born McKeesport, Pennsylvania, 1932. Received B.A. degree, University of Denver. Photographs pub-

lished: *Du* (February 1964); *Infinity* (June 1964); *Contemporary Photographer* (Spring 1964); "Duane Michals: People and Places," by Martin Fox, *Print* (March/April 1966); *Photography Annual 1967*; "The Empty Environment," *Art in America* (July/August 1967). One-man exhibitions: Underground Gallery, 1965; Art Institute of Chicago, 1968. Group exhibitions: "American Photography: The Sixties," Sheldon Memorial Art Gallery, Lincoln, Nebraska, 1966; "Contemporary Photography Since 1950," traveling exhibition prepared by George Eastman House, 1966; "Toward a Social Landscape," George Eastman House, 1966 (circulating); "Photography in the Twentieth Century," traveling exhibition prepared by the George Eastman House, 1967; "12 Photographers of the American Social Landscape," Brandeis University, Waltham, Massachusetts, 1967; "Personal Photographers," N. W. Ayer Gallery, Philadelphia, 1968; "New Acquisitions," Worcester Museum, Worcester, Massachusetts, 1968; "Photography and the City," Smithsonian Institution, Washington, D. C., 1968. Collections: Museum of Modern Art, New York City; George Eastman House; Worcester Art Museum. Address: 109 East 19th Street, New York, New York 10003.

John Mills born Madison, Wisconsin, 1941. Received A.B. and M.F.A. degrees, Indiana University. One-man exhibition: Indiana University Memorial Union Building, 1968. Group exhibitions: "Graduate Photography," Purdue University, Lafayette, Indiana, 1966; "Refocus," University of Iowa, 1966, 1967; "Young Photographers," University of New Mexico, Albuquerque, 1968; "Photography '68," Lexington Camera Club, Lexington, Kentucky, 1968. Address: Nashville, Indiana 47448.

Stephen Mindel born New York City, 1938. Received M.A. degree, San Francisco State College. Photographs published: *Hollow Orange*, Numbers 4 and 5. Address: 544 Natoma Street, San Francisco, California 94103.

David S. Moy born New York City, 1948. Currently a student at Manhattan College, Riverdale, New York. Address: 95 Elizabeth Street, New York, New York 10013.

Rodney Mullen born Puyallyp, Washington, 1943. Received B.A. degree in Political Science from the University of California at Berkeley, 1966. Studied photography with Harry Callahan, 1966. Currently graduate student at San Francisco Art Institute. Address: 5834 Birch Court, Oakland, California 94618.

Stephen S. Myers born Elmhurst, Illinois, 1942. Received B.F.A. degree, Pratt Institute, 1968. Address: 411 Vanderbilt Avenue, Brooklyn, New York 11238.

Joyce Neimanas born Chicago, Illinois, 1944. Received B.A.E. degree, School of the Art Institute of Chicago, 1966. Two-man exhibitions: Gallery Mid-North, Chicago, Illinois, 1967, 1968. Group exhibition: "FOTA," University of Chicago, 1965. Currently graduate student in photography at the School of the Art Institute of Chicago and teacher of photography at New Trier High School, Evanston, Illinois. Address: 744 Dobson Street, Evanston, Illinois 60202.

Floris Michael Neusüss born Lennep, West Germany, 1937. Studied: Bayerische Staatslehranstalt für Photographie, Munich; Hochschule für Bildende Kunste, Berlin. Photographs published: *Point de Vue, Images du Monde*, Paris, 1966; *Imago*, Kassel, 1967; *Graphic Design*, Tokyo, 1967; *Camera*, Lucerne, 1968. One-man exhibitions: Galerie des Jeunes, Paris, 1965; Galerie im Europacenter, Berlin, 1966; Galerie St. Stephan, Vienna, 1967; Galerie Clarissa, Hannover, 1968. Group exhibitions: Internationale Aktphotographie, Münchener Stadtmuseum, 1965; "11th Biennale de Paris," 1967; "Photokina 1968," Cologne, 1968. Collection: Staatliche Landesbildstelle, Hamburg; Kestner-museum, Hannover; Bayerische Staatslehranstalt für Photographie, Munich. Address: 35 Kassel, Menzelstrasse 15, West Germany.

James Newberry born Indianapolis, Indiana, 1937. Received B.S. degree, Illinois Institute of Technology. Advanced Studies Workshop, George Eastman House, 1967. Photographs published: *WFMT Guide* (January 1966); *Photography Annual,* 1966, 1968; *Trans-action* (May 1968). Group exhibitions: "FOTA," University of Chicago, 1966; Colorado Photographic Arts Center, 1966; "First National Photography Exhibition," XXth Century Gallery, Williamsburg, Virginia, 1966; "Exphotage," Chicago, 1966, 1967; "Graduate Photography," Purdue University, Lafayette, Indiana, 1966 (circulating); "Focus on the City," Rockford College, 1967; "Bytown International Exhibition," Ottawa, Canada, 1967; "Photography by Choice," East/West Gallery, Normal, Illinois, 1968. Currently Instructor of Photography, Columbia College, Chicago, Illinois. Address: 2603 Harrison Street, Evanston, Illinois 60201.

Teddy Newman born Montreal, Quebec, 1943. Studied: Sir George Williams University. Group exhibition: Saidye Bronfman Centre Staff Show, 1967. Address: 3451 Prud'homme Avenue, Montreal 28, Quebec.

Waclaw Nowak born Cracow, Poland, 1924. Graduated from the Faculty of Architecture of the Cracow Polytechnic School, 1952. Photographs published: *Fotografia,* Poland (November 1965, December 1967, January 1968); *Almanach Fotografiki Polskiej* (1959, 1960, 1962, 1964, 1967); *International Aktfotografie,* East Germany, 1966; *Fotoalmanach International,* West Germany, 1968; *Foto Arsbok 1968; Fotografie 1965,* No. 2; *Czechoslovak Fotografie,* Numbers 1 and 2, 1967; *Camera Owner,* London (March 1967); *Sovietskoye Photo,* Moscow (July 1967); *Die Fotografie,* Leipzig (May 1968). One-man exhibition: Gallery Krzysztofory, Cracow, 1968. Participant in numerous national and international exhibitions since 1957. Address: Karmelicka 55/8, Cracow, Poland.

Takayuki Ogawa born Tokyo, Japan, 1936. Received B.A. degree, Nippon University, 1959. Article about: "Two Japanese Contemporary Photographers," by Ben Watanabe, *CamerArt* (September/October 1968). Article by: "A Stay in New York," *Camera Mainichi* (September 1968). Photographs published in numerous magazines. One-man exhibitions: "New York Is," Tokyo, Japan, 1968; George Eastman House, 1969. Address: 432 Kosha Apt., 1088 Kitakase, Kawasaki, Kanagawa, Japan.

Phil Palmer born Hart, Michigan, 1911. Received B.S. degree, Michigan State University, 1932. Studied photography with Nicholas Haz. Widely published in miscellaneous national magazines in the United States from 1938 to date. One-man exhibitions: Toren Gallery, San Francisco, 1966; Focus Gallery, San Francisco, 1967; M. H. de Young Memorial Museum, San Francisco, 1968. Group exhibition: "Photography for the Arts in the Embassies," Focus Gallery and Oakland Museum, 1968. Address: 585 Gossage Avenue, Petaluma, California 94952.

Robin Panda born Detroit, Michigan, 1937. Studied: University of Toronto; McGill University, Sir George Williams College. Collection: National Film Board of Canada. Address: 3451 Prud'homme, Montreal, Quebec.

Tod Papageorge born Portsmouth, New Hampshire, 1940. Received B.A. degree in English Literature, University of New Hampshire, 1962. Studied photography with Garry Winogrand. Address: 130 East 96th Street, Apartment 4-W, New York, New York 10028.

Bart Parker born Fort Dodge, Iowa, 1934. Received B.A. degree in English Literature, University of Colorado. Studied photography with Larry Colwell and Harry Callahan. Group exhibitions: Jacksonville Arts Festival, Jacksonville, Florida, 1965; Pratt Institute, Brooklyn, 1966; Workshop 2 Gallery, Jacksonville Art Museum, 1966; "Four Photographers," Cummer Gallery of Art, Jacksonville, 1967; "Twenty-five Photographers," Cyrk Galleries, Providence, Rhode Island, 1968; Invitational Photographic Exhibition of the Rhode Island Arts Festival, Providence, 1968. Collection: Cummer Gallery of Art, Jacksonville, Florida. Address: 60 Woodbine Street, Providence, Rhode Island 02906.

Fred Parker born Compton, California, 1938. Received B.A. degree, San Francisco State College, 1964; M.A. degree, University of California at Davis, 1966. Awarded George Eastman House Work-Study Fellowship, 1968. One-man exhibitions: Belmonte Gallery, Sacramento, 1965; University of California at Davis, 1965; Powell Enterprises, Sacramento, 1965; Davis Art Center, 1968. Group exhibitions: "Kingsley Art Club Annual," Sacramento, 1965; "American Institute of Architects Invitational Exhibit," Belmonte Gallery, 1966; "33rd National Graphic Arts & Drawings Exhibition," Wichita, Kansas, 1966; "Preview '66," Benicia, Vallejo and Napa, California, 1966; "6th National Mercyhurst American Drawings," Erie Art Center, Erie, Pennsylvania, 1966; "1st Annual Festival of the Arts," University of California at Davis, 1967. Currently working as Art Director of the Memorial Union Art Gallery. Address: Memorial Union Art Gallery, University of California, Davis, Calif. 95616.

Donald Wright Patterson, Jr. born Buffalo, New York, 1937. Received B.A. degree, in Government, American University in Beirut, Lebanon and Oberlin College, 1960. Studied Economics, Oberlin College. Has been working as a free-lance photographer, journalist and film-maker. Photographs published widely, including *Life* and *Fortune.* Address: 13 Winthrop Street, Roxbury, Massachusetts 02119.

Brian Pelletier born Newport, Rhode Island, 1941. Received B.S. degree, Southeastern Massachusetts Technical Institute, 1964; M.F.A. degrees in Art Education and Photography, Rhode Island School of Design, 1968. Photograph published: *Boston Review of Photography*, No. 4 (1968). Collections: Museum of Modern Art, New York City; Art Institute of Chicago; George Eastman House. Address: 57 Admiral Kalbfus Rd., Newport, Rhode Island 02840.

Anders Petersen born Stockholm, Sweden, 1944. Photographs published: *Photography Yearbook,* Sweden, 1968, 1969; *Foto* (December 1967); *Popular Photography* (July/August 1968). Group exhibitions: "Modern Scandinavian Painting," Karlstad, Sweden, 1965; Museum of Modern Art, Stockholm, 1967. Collection: Museum of Modern Art, Stockholm. Address: c/o Kärrlander, Vällingbyvagen 90, Vällingby, Sweden.

David Pilbrow born Rochester, New York, 1940. Received B.F.A. degree, 1964, and M.F.A. degree, 1966, from Rhode Island School of Design. One-man exhibitions: St. John's Unitarian Church, Cincinnati, Ohio, 1967; Miami University, Oxford, Ohio, 1968. Group exhibitions: Institute of Design, Chicago, 1966; Southern Illinois University, 1966; "The City," Rockford College, 1967; Cincinnati Museum of Art, 1966, 1967, 1968; "Young Photographers," Purdue University, Lafayette, Indiana, 1968. Collections: Art Institute of Chicago; Museum of Modern Art, New York City. Address: 3140 Imperial Street, Cincinnati, Ohio 45220.

Thomas Porett born Chicago, Illinois, 1942. Received B.S. degree, University of Wisconsin, Madison; majored in History. Received M.S. degree, Illinois Institute of Technology. Photograph published: *Aperture,* 14:1 (1968). One-man exhibition: Lake Forest College, Lake Forest, Illinois, 1966. Group exhibition: "Light⁷," Massachusetts Institute of Technology, Cambridge, 1968. Collection: Wisconsin State Historical Society. Currently teaching photography and film at the Philadelphia College of Art and Moore College. Address: 4739 North 13th Street, Philadelphia, Pennsylvania 19141.

Walter Rabetz born Poland, 1940. Received B.A. degree, Brooklyn College, 1965. Currently candidate for M.F.A. degree, Rhode Island School of Design. Address: 31 Phillips St., Providence, Rhode Island 02906.

Nina Raginsky born Montreal, Canada, 1941. Received B.A. degree, Rutgers University, 1962. Articles about: *London Look Magazine,* January 21, 1967 and January 28, 1967; *Sunday Telegraph* (London), February 11, 1968. Photographs published: *London Weekend Telegraph Magazine,* November 25, 1966; *L'Express* (Edition Internationale, Paris, October 1966); *World Advertising Conference* (London, June 1967); *Queen Magazine* (London, Christmas, 1967); *Town Magazine* (London, October 1967); *Daily London Telegraph Magazine,* November 24, 1967; *Canada: A Year of the Land,* National Film Board of Canada, 1966-67; *Camera,* Switzerland, (April 1968). Address: 2 Westmount Square, No. 1302, Montreal 6, Quebec.

Tony Ray-Jones born Somerset, England, 1941. Received M.F.A. degree, Yale University, 1954. Studied: Alexis Brodovitch's Design Lab. Photographs published: *Creative Camera* (October 1968). Group exhibition: "Current Report 2," traveling exhibition prepared by Museum of Modern Art, New York City. Collection: Museum of Modern Art. Address: 102 Gloucester Place, London, W. 1., England.

Leland D. Rice born Los Angeles, California, 1940. Received B.S. degree, Arizona State University, 1964; M.A. degree, San Francisco State College, 1968. Workshops with Oliver Gagliani, Ruth Bernhard, Paul Caponigro. Photographs published: *Trans-action* (December 1967); *San Francisco Camera,* 1:1 (1969). Group exhibitions: "Urban Reality," SPUR of San Francisco, 1966; "Young Photographers," University of New Mexico, Albuquerque, 1968; "Definition of the New Documentary," Massachusetts Institute of Technology, Cambridge, 1968; "Young Photographers '68," Purdue University, Lafayette, Indiana, 1968. Collection: Museum of the City of San Francisco. Currently teaching photography at California College of Arts and Crafts, and President of the Visual Dialogue Foundation. Address: 996 A De Haro St., San Francisco, California 94131.

Eugene Edward Richards born Boston, Massachusetts, 1944. Received B.A. degree, Northeastern University, 1967; majored in English. Studied photography with Minor White. Photographs published: *Spectrum Literary Magazine,* Northeastern University, 1967. Group exhibitions: Harvard University, Leverett House, 1967; Massachusetts Institute of Technology, Cambridge, 1968. Address: 56 West Elm Avenue, Wollaston, Massachusetts 02170.

Robert Risager born Viborg, Denmark, 1922. Has participated in numerous international exhibitions, including: Thorvaldsens Museum, Copenhagen, 1966; and Gallery Gammel Strand, Copenhagen, 1967. Address: Agertoften 33, 2820 Gentofte, Denmark.

Murray Riss born Poland, 1940. Received B.A. degree, City University of New York; M.F.A. degree, Rhode Island School of Design. Photograph published: *Boston Review of Photography,* No. 4 (1968). One-man exhibitions: Pratt Institute, Brooklyn, New York, 1965; Bezalel School of Art, Jerusalem, Israel, 1968. Group exhibitions: Instituto Norteamericano, 1966; Rhode Island Invitational Photography Exhibit, 1968. Collections: Art Institute of Chicago; Museum of Modern Art, New York City; Sheldon Memorial Art Gallery, University of Nebraska. Currently teaching photography at the Memphis School of Fine Arts. Address: 16 Arnold Street, Providence, Rhode Island 02906.

Alvin Rosenbaum born Florence, Alabama, 1945. Received B.A. degree, Bard College,

1967. One-man exhibition: Gallery of Modern Art, Washington, D. C., 1968. Group exhibition: Touring exhibition on social problems and programs for the Model City Agency, Poughkeepsie, New York, 1968. Currently teaching a photography workshop at Bard College. Address: 33 Mill Street, Rhinebeck, New York 12572.

David Ruether born Columbus, Ohio, 1942. Studied: Cornell University; University of Oklahoma. Photographs published: *Modern Photography* (September 1966, May 1967); *Popular Photography* (October 1966); *Asahi Camera* (April 1967). One-man exhibitions: Buffalo YWCA, Buffalo, New York, 1965; Cornell University, 1965; M. H. de Young Memorial Museum, San Francisco, 1968. Group exhibitions: Ithaca College Museum, 1966, Albright-Knox Art Gallery, Buffalo, 1966. Collection: Museum of Modern Art, New York City. Address: 109 Caledonia St., Lockport, N. Y. 14094.

Linn Sage born Glyndon, Maryland, 1937. Received B.A. degree, Barnard College. Studied photography with Paul Hassel, Lisette Model, Bruce Davidson. Photographs published: "West 114th Street," pamphlet published by the Office of Economic Opportunity, 1966. Group exhibition: Camera Club of New York, 1967. Address: c/o Rulon-Miller, 322 Central Park West, New York, New York 10025.

Michael Saint-Jean born Montreal, Canada, 1937. Studied: Ecole Supérieure Saint-Viateur and Ecole des Beaux-Arts de Montréal. Photographs published: *La Presse; Maclean; Chatelaine; Perspectives; Weekend; The Canadian; Culture Vivante; Objectif; Cahiers du Cinema; Cimaise; Foto Canada.* Group exhibitions: "Graphica '65," Montreal, 1965; "Montreal Insolite," La Bibliothèque Nationale, Montreal, 1967; "Anti-Erotic Erotica," Review Theater, Montreal, 1968; "Unusual Montreal," Pascal Gallery, Toronto, 1968; "Photography in Canada 1967," Canadian Government Photo Center Gallery, Ottawa, 1968; "Graphica '68," Toronto, 1968. Numerous exhibition awards. Collections:

National Film Board of Canada; La Place des Arts, Montreal. Address: 10 East, Gouin Boulevard, Montreal 12, Quebec.

Frank Salmo born Herrin, Illinois, 1942. Received B.S. degree, Southern Illinois University, 1965; M.F.A. degree, Ohio University, 1968. Photograph published: *Photography Annual 1969.* Group exhibition: Zanesville Art Institute, Zanesville, Ohio, 1967. Currently Instructor of Photography, University of Hawaii, Honolulu. Address: c/o Angelo Salmo, 716 North Park Avenue, Herrin, Illinois 62948.

Serge A. Scherbatskoy born Tulsa, Oklahoma, 1945. Received B.A. degree in Philosophy, Reed College, Portland, Oregon, 1966. Studied photography with Ralph Hattersley, Brett Weston, Imogene Cunningham, Jack Welpott. Photographs published: *San Francisco Camera*, 1:1 (1969). Two-man exhibition: Reed College, 1968. Currently graduate student in photography at San Francisco State College. Address: 874 Page, No. 4, San Francisco, Cal. 94117.

Michael Semak born Welland, Canada, 1934. Studied: University of Toronto. Received Architectural Technology Diploma from Ryerson Institute of Technology. Photographs published: *Modern Photography* (1965); *Trans-action* (1967, 1968); in various publications of the National Film Board of Canada. Group exhibitions: "International Press Photo Exhibition," Moscow, 1966; "Bytown International," Ottawa, 1967; "This City Now," Art Gallery, 1967; "If This is the Time," National Film Board, Ottawa, 1969. Recipient of Canadian Federal Government grant for travel to Tunisia, Ghana, Paris, Sierra Leone. Collection: National Film Board of Canada. Address: 22 Pakenham Drive, Rexdale, Ontario.

Lawrence L. Simon born Philadelphia, Pennsylvania, 1943. Received B.F.A. degree, Philadelphia College of Art. Group exhibitions: Cheltenham Art Center, 1965, 1967. Address: 9 West Tultehocken Street, Philadelphia, Pennsylvania 19144.

Leif Skoogfors born Wilmington, Delaware, 1940. Studied: Alexis Brodovitch's Design Laboratory. Photographs published in *Newsweek, Trans-action* and other magazines. One-man exhibition: Philadelphia Art Alliance, 1966. Group exhibitions: Vanderlip Gallery, Philadelphia, 1967, 1969. Currently Head of Photography Department, Moore College of Art. Address: 1629 Chestnut Street, Philadelphia, Pennsylvania 19103.

Keith A. Smith born Indiana, 1938. Received B.A.E. degree, School of the Art Institute of Chicago, 1967; M.S. degree, Illinois Institute of Technology, 1968. One-man exhibition: Art Institute of Chicago, 1968. Group exhibitions: "FOTA," University of Chicago, 1965, 1966; "Chicago and Vicinity Print and Drawing Show," Art Institute of Chicago, 1966. Collections: Museum of Modern Art, New York City; Museum of Greelong, Victoria, Australia. Currently teaching drawing and painting at Morton East High School, Cicero, Illinois. Address: 1409½ North Wells Street, Chicago, Illinois 60610.

Philip L. Smith born Brooklyn, New York, 1939. Received B.A. degree, Brooklyn College, 1961; M.A. degree, San Francisco State College, 1967. Workshop with Ansel Adams, Wynn Bullock, Brett Wilson, Blair Stapp, and Morley Baer, 1966; with Harry Callahan, 1966. One-man exhibitions: Music and Art Institute of San Francisco, 1967; San Francisco State College Library, 1967. Group exhibitions: Herald Gallery, San Francisco, 1965, "Urban Reality," SPUR of San Francisco, 1966; San Francisco State College, 1966; "Photography '66," University of Santa Clara, 1966; Focus Gallery, 1967; "Young Photographers," University of New Mexico, Albuquerque, 1968. Address: 709 Bruno Avenue, San Francisco, California 94107.

Egons Spuris born Riga, Latvia, 1931. Self-taught as a photographer. Photographs published: *Photoalmanach International,* 1968, 1969. Participant in numerous international photographic exhibitions. Address: Riga 9 Sarkanarmi 73 b 49, Latvia, USSR.

Jon Ellis Stevens born Syracuse, New York, 1944. Received B.S. degree in Art Education, State University of New York at New Paltz. Two-man exhibition: The Regent Theater, 1967. Address: 104 Woods Road, North Syracuse, New York 13212.

J. Douglas Stewart born Ann Arbor, Michigan, 1931. Received B.S. degree, University of Michigan, 1955; M.F.A. degree, Ohio University, 1967. One-man exhibitions: Otterbein College, Ohio, 1968; Lake Erie College, Ohio, 1968. Two-man exhibition: Zanesville Art Institute, Zanesville, Ohio, 1967. Numerous group exhibitions, including "Young Photographers '68," Purdue University, Lafayette, Indiana, 1968. Collections: Museum of Modern Art, New York City; Columbus Gallery of Fine Arts, Columbus, Ohio; Zanesville Art Institute, Zanesville, Ohio; Otterbein College, Westerville, Ohio. Address: 817-C Greenbriar, De Kalb, Illinois 60115.

Michael J. Teres born Brooklyn, New York, 1940. Received B.A. degree, Hunter College, 1962; M.A. degree, 1965, and M.F.A. degree, 1966, University of Iowa. Photographs published: *Aperture,* 14:1 (1968); *Camera.* One-man exhibitions: St. Benedict's College, 1966; University of Florida, 1967. Group exhibitions: University of Saskatchewan, 1965; Moorhead State College, 1965. "Midwest Photographers," 1966 (traveling exhibition); "Photography USA," De Cordova Museum, Lincoln, Massachusetts, 1968; "Light⁷," Massachusetts Institute of Technology, Cambridge, 1968. Collection: George Eastman House. Currently Assistant Professor of Photography at the State University College at Geneseo, New York. Address: 43 Oak Street, Geneseo, New York 14454.

Ron Testa born Youngstown, Ohio, 1942. Received B.F.A. degree, Cleveland Institute of Art. Group exhibitions: "May Show,"

Cleveland Museum of Art, 1965, 1966; Cleveland Jewish Community Center Photography Show, 1965, 1966; Lake Erie College for Women, 1965. Address: USS Ticonderoga (CVA-14), F.P.O. San Francisco, California 96601.

Haruo Tomiyama born Tokyo, Japan, 1936. Photographs published: *Camera Mainichi* (September 1966); *Asahi Graph; Asahi Journal; Shukan Asahi.* One-man exhibition: "Essay of the Modern Society," Tokyo, 1965. Collection: National Museum of Modern Art, Tokyo. Address: 7, Saneicho, Shinjuku-ku, Tokyo, Japan.

Arthur Tress born Brooklyn, New York, 1940. Received B.S.A. degree, Bard College. Photographs published: *Foto och Film Technique,* Sweden (November, December 1967); *Fotografiske Arsbok,* Sweden (1968); *Photography,* England (March 1968); *Creative Camera,* No. 45 (March 1968); *Popular Fotografie,* Sweden (February 1968). Address: 46 Riverside Drive, New York, New York 10024.

Burk Uzzle born Raleigh, North Carolina, 1938. Studied photography with Gjon Mili. Became a member of Magnum. Photographs published: *Creative Camera,* No. 48 (June 1968); *Infinity,* 16:11 (1967); *Photography Annual,* 1965, 1966, 1968, 1969; in *Life* magazine and in numerous European periodicals. One-man exhibition: Photography/Cinematography, Roxbury, Massachusetts, 1969. Collections: Museum of Modern Art, New York City; Smithsonian Institution, Washington, D. C.; Metropolitan Museum of Art. Address: c/o Magnum Photos, 72 West 45th Street, New York, New York 10036.

Pavel Vácha born Prague, Czechoslovakia, 1940. Studied: Film Faculty of the Academy of Musical Arts in Prague. Photographs published: *Czechoslovak Fotografie* and in weekly magazines. Group exhibitions: "World Press Photo Exhibition," Haag, 1966, 1968; Exposition of Czechoslovakian photoreporters, 1965, 1968. Independent exhibitions in Prague, 1965, 1968. Address: Na Petynce 32, Prague 6, Czechoslovakia.

David Vestal born California, 1924. Became actively interested in photography, 1947. Studied with Ansel Adams, Sid Grossman, Evsa Model. Appointed Dean of New York Institute of Photography 1965. Articles and photographs published: *U. S. Camera* (February 1964); *Infinity* (March, September 1963; March 1964), May, (1968); *Popular Photography* (January, March, April, May, July, August, November, December 1964; January 1965); *Photography Annual 1968.* Participant in numerous one-man and group exhibitions since 1954. Awarded Guggenheim Fellowship, 1966. Collections: Museum of Modern Art, New York City; Art Institute of Chicago. Currently Associate Editor of *Popular Photography.* Address: 715 Carroll Street, Brooklyn, New York 11215.

Gary Viskupic born Brooklyn, New York, 1944. Received B.F.A. degree, Cooper Union, 1965; M.F.A. degree, University of Illinois, 1968. Group exhibition: "Young Photographers," University of New Mexico, Albuquerque, 1968. Address: 1657 Deer Park Avenue, Deer Park, Long Island, New York 11729.

Wolf von dem Bussche born Pforzheim, Germany, 1934. Studied: Columbia College, 1956-62. Photographs published: *U. S. Camera* (May 1968); *New York State Council on the Arts 1967-68 Annual Report; Genre of Silence* (St. Mark's Press, 1967); *New York Times Magazine,* March 3, 1968; *Image* (July 1968); *American Heritage,* Volume 12, "American Presidents"; *Fortune; Newsweek; Dance Magazine.* Group exhibitions: "The People Protest," Crypt Gallery, Columbia University, 1967; "Photography USA," De Cordova Museum, Lincoln, Massachusetts, 1968. Address: 46 West 90th St., New York, N. Y. 10024.

John Spence Weir born Los Angeles, California, 1930. Received B.A. degree, San

Francisco State College. Photographs published: *San Francisco Camera,* 1:1 (1969). Group exhibitions: "Urban Reality," SPUR of San Francisco, 1966; "233.03 Group," Focus Gallery, San Francisco, 1967; "Young Photographers," University of New Mexico, Albuquerque, 1968; "Documentary Day Exhibition," Massachusetts Institute of Technology, Cambridge, 1968. Currently a graduate student at San Francisco State College. Address: 888 Waller Street, San Francisco, California 94117.

Henry Wessel, Jr. born Teaneck, New Jersey, 1942. Received B.A. degree, Pennsylvania State University, 1965. Group exhibitions: "Central Pennsylvania Festival of the Arts," 1968; "Photographs," Pennsylvania State University, 1968; "Four Photographers," Gorham State College, Gorham, Maine, 1968. Currently Instructor of Photography at University of Pennsylvania. Address: P. O. Box 77, Boalsburg, Pennsylvania 16827.

Paul J. Wigger born Massena, New York, 1942. Received B.S. degree, State University of New York at Buffalo, 1965; M.A. and M.F.A. degrees, University of Iowa, 1968. Group exhibitions: "First Annual Photographic Exhibition," 20th Century Gallery, Williamsburg, Virginia, 1966; Davenport Art Center, Davenport, Iowa, 1966; "Young Photographers," University of New Mexico, Albuquerque, 1967, 1968; "Young Photographers '68," Purdue University, Lafayette, Indiana, 1968; "Light⁷," Massachusetts Institute of Technology, 1968. Collections: Art Institute of Chicago; Massachusetts Institute of Technology. Address: 601 South Lucas, Iowa City, Iowa 52240.

Jack F. Wilgus born Chicago, Illinois, 1943. Received B.F.A. degree, School of the Art Institute of Chicago, 1965; M.S. degree, Illinois Institute of Technology, 1967. Group exhibitions: "FOTA," University of Chicago, 1966; "Graduate Photography," Purdue University, Lafayette, Indiana, 1966; "Refocus," University of Iowa, 1966, 1967; "Graduate Photography," Iowa State

University, 1967; "Young Photographers," University of New Mexico, Albuquerque, 1968; Friends of Photography Gallery, Carmel, California, 1968; "Image 68," Kovler Gallery, Chicago, 1968. Currently teaching photography at the Maryland Institute College of Art. Address: 4926 Bowland Avenue, Baltimore, Maryland 21206.

Ann Warrington Wills born Cincinnati, Ohio, 1944. Received B.A. degree, Boston University, 1966. Photographs published: *Boston Review of Photography,* No. 1 (1967); *Aperture,* 14:1 (1968). Article by: *Boston Review of Photography,* No. 1 (1967). One-man exhibition: Cary Library, Lexington, Massachusetts, 1967. Group exhibitions: Massachusetts Institute of Technology, 1967; Cambridge Artists Association, 1967; Cohasset Arts Festival, 1967; Club 47, Cambridge, Massachusetts, 1967, "Light⁷," Massachusetts Institute of Technology, Cambridge, 1968. Address: 2260 Riverview St., Eugene, Oregon 97403.

William A. Winans born New Rochelle, New York, 1943. Received A.B. degree, Wesleyan University, 1965. Fulbright Grant to University of Freiburg, Germany, 1965-66. Address: 4377 17th Street, San Francisco, California 94114.

Geoffrey L. Winningham born Jackson, Tennessee, 1943. Received B.A. degree in English, Rice University; M.S. degree, Illinois Institute of Technology. Photographs published: *Photography Annual 1969.* Group exhibitions: Memorial Center Gallery, Rice University, 1967; Friends of Photography Gallery, Carmel, California, 1968. Currently Assistant Professor at Media Center at the University of St. Thomas, Houston, Texas. Address: Univ. of St. Thomas, Houston, Texas 77006.

John Wood born Delhi, California, 1922. Received B.S. degree, Illinois Institute of Technology, 1954. One-man exhibitions: State University of New York at Brockport, 1965; State University of New York at Cortland, 1966; Edinboro State College, Edin-

boro, Pennsylvania, 1966; Kendall Gallery, Wellfleet, Massachusetts, 1966; Schuman Gallery, Rochester, New York, 1968. Group exhibitions: Albright-Knox Art Gallery, Buffalo, 1965; Memorial Art Gallery, Rochester, 1965, New York State Council on the Arts, 1965; "Contemporary Photography Since 1950," traveling exhibition prepared by George Eastman House; "Photography in the Twentieth Century," traveling exhibition prepared by George Eastman House, 1967; State University Faculty Exhibition, Albright-Knox Art Gallery, 1967; "The Persistence of Vision," George Eastman House, 1967 (circulating); "Five Photographers," Sheldon Memorial Art Gallery, University of Nebraska, Lincoln, 1968. Currently Associate Professor of Design at New York State College of Ceramics, Alfred University. Address: Alfred, New York 14802.

Myron Wood born Wilson, Oklahoma, 1921. Received B.F.A. degree in Music. Studied photography with Edward Weston and Roy Stryker, and at the Progressive School of Photography, New Haven, Connecticut. Photographs published in numerous periodicals, including: *Time, Fortune, Business Week,* and *The New York Times.* Group exhibitions: "Expo '67," Montreal, 1967; Metropolitan Museum, New York City, 1967. Awarded grant from Bonfils Foundation to photograph in Colorado. Address: 825 Paseo, Colorado Springs, Colorado 80907.

Tom Zimmerman born Brooklyn, New York, 1938. Photograph published: *Museum of Modern Art Calendar,* 1967. One-man exhibition: "Phil's Wall," New York City, 1967. Group exhibitions: Museum of Modern Art, New York City, 1966; "12 Photographers of the American Social Landscape," Brandeis University, Waltham, Massachusetts, 1967; "Contemporary Photography Since 1950," traveling exhibition prepared by George Eastman House. Collections: Museum of Modern Art, New York City; George Eastman House. Address: 160 South Main Street, New Hope, Pennsylvania 18938.